CHAMPIONSHIP
DRIVE

A NOVEL

SARAH BETH AUBREY

ISBN: 978-1-48356-683-2 (Print)
ISBN: 978-1-48356-684-9 (eBook)

Author's Note

Dear Reader,

  Championship Drive is a work of fiction. Many of *you* will undoubtedly feel as though you 'know' one character or another in this book. We are an industry of characters, aren't we? There are many commonalities that bind us together in this crazy livestock-showing business. Still, the characters in **Championship Drive** are fictional and don't represent any real-life person or group of persons. They are each of my own creation. I welcome you to enjoy the antics of these colorful cattle-showing men and women, picturing each as you will in your own mind.

Sarah Beth Aubrey
December 2015

To Cary,
I'm grateful for every day that we walk the tan bark together.
ILU And SSW.

Tying In

'Tying in' is an active phrase. It's both a verb and an adjective describing the act of leading cattle back to the stalls. To 'tie in' signifies the beginning of a new day. It means whirring fans, feeding time, uncoiling the blower hose, and finding a wash rack spot.

Whatever happened yesterday is done.

It's on that walk in that you allow hope and possibility. You think about the chance to impress the right potential customer. You think about laughing with your friends. You think about just how good the stock look this time out.

You entertain that powerful dream – *you could win today.*

Tying in doesn't make sense unless you've done it so many times that you could lead two in each hand - in your sleep – and probably have. It's automatic. So, to understand what that morning walk through mud or sleet, blowing snow or stifling humidity means, well, you just know the feeling - or you don't.

It is a cow show thing.

PROLOGUE

Kansas City, MO

October 1999

Grand Champion Drive

She'd never forget the sounds from that day. Sounds at a cattle show permeate everything. The constant hum of fans, the way a boot heel clicks on a blower switch, the pop of the thousandth beer can being opened somewhere in the aisle all seem to become part of the brain, like ringing in the ears.

She would remember the soft, sure thud of her heifer's hooves striding out along her right, the show halter clinking softly, leather against metal neck chain. She could hear the rustle of her starched jeans as the cuffs rubbed along her ostrich boots. The big bred was long broke. She barely had to lead her. They walked together, heads high, eyes defiant, hearts hopeful. As Savannah pulled her into the championship drive line up, she knew they were in the hunt. She heard the whispery, scratching sound of the show stick along Tiara's brisket, the gentle scratching of her chin calming them both. Savannah felt her heart pound and listened to the rasp of their shared breathing. They posed, unmoving, as the judge made his final pass…

"Welcome to your 100th National Show! Hereford Show exhibitors are now in the ring showing for Grand Champion Female!" bellowed the announcer as Savannah watched the judge approach the microphone.

She scanned the ring. A few nervous types were circling their heifers yet again. The people standing down in second place looked bored. She saw her mother, Jessica, with digital camera aimed. It was odd that she came, Savannah mused. She'd seen her parents arguing earlier in the day, though that was typical since they'd been separated for years.

"The opportunity to evaluate your National Show and look at a set of females of this caliber is an honor I'm humbled to accept," the judge was saying. He was already into the standard Grand Champion Drive Speech for a good three or four minutes, but he continued on, enjoying his time at the mic. "Let's have another round of applause for the exhibitors and more importantly the breeders of these females. I'll go show ya'll a champion."

Savannah searched for her Dad at the ringside, but was distracted; the judge had begun his brisk walk toward the inevitable winner. She straightened, lengthened her lead arm, and gently urged the heifer's head up and out. Savannah stared intently at the tall, lean man in clad in a cowboy hat and crisply starched Wrangler Riata's. We was pacing the ring a lot, going nearly up to one heifer only to pass her by. He put his head down and walked back out into the center of ring as if he needed more time to contemplate. Abruptly, he turned, moving purposefully in Savannah's direction.

Then she heard Jessica Morgan scream.

PART I

Independence

~ ONE ~

Twilight

At the farm, Late October 1999

The screen door slammed with a rapid bang. Ordinarily, she would have eased it shut but Savannah barely noticed the clattering noise. She sat down and took a sip of her drink, whiskey, straight, the way her Dad had liked it.

She watched the spreading red stain of horizon as the chilling wind blew in from the North, billowing her Columbia puffer. Savannah zipped it, knowing soon the fall would give way to winter. She took another healthy sip of Crown Royal, cringing as it forged its way down her throat.

How am I going to get through winter and calving season without Dad?

A week ago thinking of Harlan Morgan probably would have ticked her off, strained as their relationship was most of the time. They'd even argued about whether or not the big heifer, Tiara, should have gone to Kansas City. But that annoyance was replaced with grief. Last Sunday's stunning news that Harlan had fallen dead had shocked her, but now her sore, red-rimmed eyes were cried out.

She had decisions to make.

She had inherited the cattle farm and the life's work she'd always known in her heart was hers. Savannah was in charge and though she'd spent her entire 24 years learning, she had no idea what to do next.

Savannah was tall, nearly six feet without shoes. Grateful, at least, to be back in a pair of faded Rockies jeans and an old sweatshirt, she extended her long legs off the top porch step, stretching as she irritably massaged her temples.

"Savannah, are you out there?" called Troy Howell.

She stiffened, but pretended not to hear. He'd be ready to head back to their home in town.

Troy stepped into the increasingly brisk evening. He rolled his eyes and sighed impatiently as if waiting for Savannah to acknowledge his presence. She knew he was there but had nothing to say.

"Savannah! I've been on the phone with your Dad's attorney. He called again. I went ahead and made arrangements to meet with him tomorrow. I have been taking care of what needs to be done and here you are just sitting around getting drunk. If you're going to do that, at least do it where people can't see," he added, clearly annoyed.

There was no one to see; the Morgan place was on its own road. Savannah didn't care enough about Troy anymore to bother getting angry. Her emotions were spent, her body drained. "Troy," she began, "all the funeral guests have left and we're the only ones here. I'll drink on my front porch if I want to."

Troy clenched his small, soft hands into fists. He was losing patience with his wife but fighting would make her stubborn; he'd worked very hard this weekend to be nice, but the imitation kindness was fast eroding.

"Savannah, please don't be so obnoxious. Anyway, I've gotten an appointment for us to meet your attorney tomorrow at 9:00 to begin moving all the property to your name. Sad as you are you don't want to be hungover, too!" Troy laughed at his joke. Then, seeing that he had made no impression, he added, "I have to say, you look like crap already, Hon. This funeral and crying has made you look rough. No offense."

Savannah drained the last of the Crown Royal in one gulp. Standing, she turned to face Troy. She was about an inch taller than him, even without rising to her full height. Standing next to Troy always made her feel powerful. She knew his secret; he tried to hide his self-conscious shortcomings by constantly making cruel remarks under the guise of kidding. He'd done it for as long as she could remember. Savannah bent her head forward, emphasizing her stature and looked through him.

Why have I stayed married?

Troy fidgeted under her unseeing gaze and stepped back a pace.

"What?" he managed to say, recovering his impatience and attempting to dominate her by standing up taller.

"I'm going for a walk and I'm staying here tonight. I'll see you in town tomorrow," she said and without releasing his gaze, she set her empty tumbler in his hand and strode off the porch.

"Come-on, Rory!" Savannah had to call out only once to alert the Australian Shepard to her presence. The dog bounded around the corner from the garage looking as if he'd missed an opportunity. Rory was always ready to work cows. Savannah petted her dog affectionately and the two turned north towards a nearly deserted country lane that connected the sections of Morgan Cattle Company.

Troy watched her with a grimace. She had a nice rear end, but there were lots well-built women out there, not that he could get many to notice him. Troy might look and he'd love to touch, but he'd never leave Savannah Morgan for another woman. She had what other women around his hometown didn't; access to land, valuable potential development land, which in Troy's view, meant access to money. He'd been dreaming for years about how much he could get for the old Morgan place when Savannah finally inherited it. But he hadn't bargained on the stroke of luck like her old man kicking off when he did.

Savannah was less than a quarter mile up the lane when she heard Troy speeding out of the driveway. "What a relief to be rid of him for the night," she said aloud. "What's his deal this week anyway?" she continued talking to herself as she forged her way into the late fall wind. Rory loped on ahead, the sound of his collar tags tinkling lightly as he moved out.

As Savannah entered the field that led down to the woods, the wind blasted her with enough force that she stumbled. Wishing she had grabbed a band for her long hair, she swept the now-tangled blonde mess out of her face and tried without success to pin it behind her ears. The cold wind brought her thoughts back to the present and her situation. She had to think. Rory was already far ahead in the 50-acre woods that ran along the White River. His tawny coat just matched the color of the leaf-strewn ground.

Savannah made her way to the gate, opened the creaking device and pulled it shut. As she moved from the treeless hilltop of the hay field to the encompassing cover of the woods, the wind nearly ceased. All around her were the Hereford cows she loved. They grazed demurely along the river's edge, completely unbothered by her approach. Most were successful old show heifers and could be petted or even haltered in the field. Unconsciously, Savannah noted that summer's grass was fast disappearing.

It won't be long before we'll need to put out hay, I had better talk with Dad about moving some round bales up from the south place, she thought.

Realizing immediately that her Dad was not there to tell, Savannah felt her knees weaken and she sunk to a tree stump. Tears came without effort and momentarily Savannah covered her face with her long, slender fingers and wept loudly.

Savannah's wails were piercing enough to finally disturb the mama cows grazing in the dusk light. When she lifted her head, Rory looked abject and the cows had stopped foraging and were gazing with overt curiosity. In spite of it all, she managed to laugh.

"You girls must think I'm crazy!" She offered Rory a pat on the head that he accepted heartily as he plopped from his haunches to his belly. The cows were soon disinterested and began to ramble as she sat, calmed. The dimming light cloaked the woods in a mauve hue. She observed the tall walnut grove, saw the last of the leaves swirling to the ground, watched the river for a moment, its slow amble through her woods on its way South through the Indiana. She heard the night birds start their song and even a screech owl with its eerie call.

She was suddenly confident about what she had to do.

Troy, of course, had said her only option was to sell the place and start immediately collecting cash by liquidating cattle. But Savannah rejected that idea again with renewed energy. This was her family's land! Savannah wasn't going to sell out just because she was afraid about managing it. *She* would stay and raise the cows, go to the shows, market the calves, and run the farm. In the three years since she'd graduated from college, Savannah had been dreaming most every weekday morning about what it would be like to wake up and know that she didn't have to go into town. Her job as an insurance underwriter paid well, but it was boring and she hated it. Tomorrow, she'd give her two weeks at work and have the painful argument with Troy about her decision. He wouldn't accept it; maybe that would be enough to entice him to leave.

Savannah stood up, now engulfed in an almost purple darkness. It would be pitch black by the time she walked back to the house, but she didn't care. She knew her way around this old place; it was home.

~ TWO ~

Prelude to Independence

"Savvy, dear!" Troy announced when she entered the downtown Indianapolis offices of Madsen and Madsen. "How did you sleep, Sweetie?" he asked while steering her towards an overstuffed leather chair. Troy being both early and chipper was suspicious.

"Here, sit down. I thought we'd get organized first, so I asked your Dad's lawyer to give us fifteen minutes before he came in and read the will and you started signing stuff over," Troy continued, as usual without waiting for Savannah to answer. Pausing to sip his coffee, he visually appraised her. "Oh, Savannah, you've worn you're hair back, you know how I hate that! It really makes your forehead look big, no offense," he added, shaking his head as if Savannah had done something completely stupid.

She sighed, took a seat, and folded her hands neatly. Offering Troy an imitation of the patronizing smile he wore, she spoke. "To answer your first question, not that you care, I was up almost the entire night planning and working through what I am going to do. I have some things to discuss with you, but I don't need your help deciding what to do with the farm."

"Well, that's a relief," Troy chortled, plopping himself into a big navy chair. "I'm glad to know you didn't just spend the evening sitting around looking at old pictures and mooning over some stupid idea about staying on the farm. I've already contacted the assessor's office and fortunately we can parcel out the property into as small as five acre tracts..."

"Troy, I'm not selling my family's property."

"Savannah, don't be ridiculous. There is *no other option*," he stated, arranging his expression into his characteristic smirk that revealed small, unevenly spaced teeth. "I know you like showing cows, but you should have put that hobby behind you after 4-H. It is time to move on. I'll go ask for Madsen," Troy finished as if since he'd spoken further conversation was mute.

Savannah let him leave. He could think what he wanted to, but she wasn't budging. Savannah glanced around the conference room absently noting the heavy, dark wood paneling and the corporate standard emerald green, burgundy, and navy motif common to offices that wanted to appear stately, stuffy, or intimidating. This place seemed an odd location to discuss the future of her family's farm. Her father was a cattleman and would have been uncomfortable sitting in the pretentious environment. She had always envisioned the farm transition as something that happened far down the road, when *she* was her Dad's age, not 24. She had known for several years that she would inherit the farm if either of her parents passed away-it was one arrangement that the sparring elder Morgan's had agreed upon. But, she never expected to deal with it so soon. Instead, she had hoped to join her father in some kind of partnership, if they could manage to get along, but she never intended to replace him! Now she was in the office of an attorney she barely knew and Troy was plotting her land sale prospects the day after her dad was buried.

Life was coming at Savannah fast.

"Savannah, I'm Roland Madsen. We've met a few times before," began the attorney as he entered the room, extending his hand. He was a big man, white haired and robust with a barrel chest and yet fit body as if he kayaked or ran to stay lean. He sported a massive diamond ring on his right hand. "I'd like to say 'its my pleasure' but dealing with an estate in an untimely manner is never a pleasure. I'm so sorry about your father, Savannah. He was a fine man, and a friend."

Savannah took a seat. "I'm sorry my mother isn't here, but sometimes she avoids these kinds of conversations where Dad is concerned."

"Oh, that's no worry at all. You know your mother, her input has been part of the estate plan all along," Madsen said. Evidently he knew Jessica Morgan well enough to appreciate her professional intellect.

"I appreciate your condolences, but let's get on with this business," she said.

"Finally, something my wife and I agree on!" announced Troy.

Madsen ignored him, directing his attention solely to Savannah. "Well, your parents set the property up in trust for you. As you know, the original parcel was your mother's ground and the balance they built jointly over the years. When they separated a few years ago, they came to see me and we made some changes. They set it up so that if either of them passed, you would inherit the use of it and all of the income from the property. However, you are not be able to sell it for five years from the date of transfer. Your mother will have the title until then. You may run it as you wish and do with the income as you wish, but again, you won't be able to sell it for five years," finished Madsen.

Savannah's reaction was delayed, but Troy's wasn't. "What the hell do you mean, Madsen? Her dad always said that the land would go to her even though her mother might still be living! There's got to be some mistake!"

"There's no mistake, Mr. Howell," Madsen began but was immediately cut off as Troy leapt to his feet and began pacing nervously, wringing his small hands in agitation. His already pasty face was white as a sheet. His temples thumped noticeably.

"Troy, what's the matter with you?" Savannah was exasperated at his rudeness. "I did inherit the land, but this way Mom and Dad solved the argument between us that I'd been dreading all week. Now that I can't sell it, you won't have to push me to do something that I would never do anyway." Savannah was smug, but for reassurance she glanced at the attorney. "Right, Mr. Madsen?"

Madsen smiled. He was clearly pleased about disrupting Troy's plans to sell the Morgan place. "That's correct. You can keep the revenue off the place, but you can't sell the land or subdivide it unless your mother signs off on it. It's secure," he added with a wink.

Savannah allowed a small smile. Finally something *her parents* agreed on.

Troy exploded with rage and began to rant, flailing his arms in violent gestures. "Savannah," he hissed as his face went from pallid to flushed. "You did this! You and your father did this as some stupid plan for you to be a little cowgirl! It's ridiculous! Damn stupid! There is no way to make money with show cattle!" Troy's hateful expression surprised both Madsen and Savannah. He suddenly advanced on her with a malicious look. "It's all about development! We live near Indy-this ground is valuable! Are you an idiot?" he shrieked.

Troy beat his palms against the heaving conference room table. "You're going to break us running that dump! It's so dumb-" Troy was cut off by two security guards lumbering through the door. They grabbed him under each arm so quickly he had no time to react.

"What the-" Troy jumped, going from furious to terrified.

"Easy boys!" he whined.

"Mr. Howell, I cannot permit this behavior in my office or in the company of your wife who is clearly innocent of the claims you are making. You'll be escorted to the parking lot and we don't expect to see you in our offices again without invitation," Madsen turned to watch the security guards drag the stunned and sniveling Troy out of the room.

"I'm sorry, Savannah, I just can't tolerate rude behavior. We can take care of this with out your husband, anyway," said Madsen as he spread a stack of papers across the table.

Savannah was so shocked that she laughed. "Mr. Madsen, I can appreciate your lack of tolerance for Troy, he can be a jerk. My dad didn't like him much either, though he never mentioned it."

A sly smile piqued the corners of Madsen's full lips. "Oh, he mentioned it."

Savannah nodded knowingly. "I shouldn't be surprised, Mom and Dad always knew we wouldn't last."

Madsen reached inside his suit jacket for a gold-plated pen. "Not for much longer, anyway."

———— • ◆ • ————

Conveniently, Madsen's law offices were housed in the same 36-story building as Savannah's insurance office. After the long night of pondering, planning, and outright praying Savannah was armed with a plan to make her exit go smoothly for the company, but knowing the man she worked for it still might not be easy. She was glad that she'd worn her best suit. The bright red tailored jacket was slimming and the skirt fit just right. She wore best jewelry, with the exception of wedding rings; they'd been in the safe for months under the guise that she didn't want to get them dirty working at the farm.

Knowing her boss wouldn't expect her due to bereavement leave, she decided the element of surprise might be useful. Upon entering the office, he welcomed her with pleasure noting how resilient she was to come back into work earlier than expected. But when she asked to speak with him privately and then offered two weeks notice and working from home for a month to help transition her projects to another account manger, his goodwill immediately faded.

"You've got to be kidding me, Savannah!" Bart Stanley began. "You can't work from home any more that you can quit! You've got some of our most important projects to finish up! How dare you consider leaving!" He stood up and slammed his palms on the desk.

Unfortunately for Bart, Savannah's tolerance for overbearing, self-serving men had already reached its daily maximum. She watched silently as he raged about her irresponsibility, lack of work ethic, and as he proclaimed the bind she was leaving him in. He carried on about her gall at 'hanging him out to dry'. As she endured the tirade, Savannah pretended she was watching a play from Stage Right while she, the supporting actress, awaited her cue. She had always thought Bart's mouth looked a piranha's - a grey whole with little yellow cigarette-stained teeth poking out of it. He was just gross.

Again she found herself wondering why she had tolerated the negative presence of men like Bart Stanley and Troy Howell for so long. Harlan's death had already taught her something serious - *what mattered*. Working for the Bart Stanley's of the world did not matter.

Savannah knew she'd burn a bridge, but she just couldn't ignore her compulsion to do it. Not allowing Bart to finish his pity parade, Savannah rose and left his office, stopping only to tell his indignant and overly perfumed secretary that she would e-mail a resignation letter and that she'd like her final paycheck direct deposited.

Savannah left the cement high rise and yanking her hair from the bun and unbuttoning her blazer, she headed home.

She was never coming back to the office in town again.

———— • ◆ • ————

Savannah drank coffee as she willed herself to wake up and face the day. For the first of November it was a pretty morning; the sun brought warm rays into the kitchen, spilling light streaks across the familiar space.

The reality of her decisions was beginning to weigh heavily. She had so much to do: deal with Troy, find time to move her things to the farm, and most importantly, go through everything in her Dad's office-probably the task she dreaded most of all. Harlan has always been secretive about money acting like it was never any of her business. She had a vague worry about the state of the finances already.

Savannah's thoughts were interrupted by the sound of a pickup and Rory's bark. Savannah glanced at her watch: 10:45. Her neighbor and old friend, Eddie Quiggly, was not one to get in a hurry about doing chores, but it was practically noon.

I'll take over chores tomorrow morning, she vowed.

Heading to the mudroom, she pulled on a well-worn pair of 36-inseam Wrangler '5-pockets', a sweatshirt and old boots. She had to talk with Eddie about setting up some kind of arrangement to get the big heifer, Tiara, ready for the Louisville, Kentucky show. People would be expecting her to sit it out because of Harlan's death, but Savannah was planning on going – and winning. That she was so close in Kansas City and shut out was hard to take. If she didn't try again, in light of everything, she would feel even more defeated.

As Savannah and Rory strode out to the barnlot, she noticed Eddie's new white truck, the sunlight glinting intensely off its shiny chrome accents giving the F250 a sparkling appearance. It was detailed perfectly - not a spot of mud on it. Savannah wondered where he got the money for a brand new truck when he always had time to loaf. Eddie was often in between factory jobs, but his relatively light employment schedule had been to Savannah's advantage; he'd been taking care of chores since Sunday.

She and Eddie were high school classmates and her dad used Eddie's help on and off for basic stuff like mowing hay or breaking show calves. Though a below average cowhand prone to bouts of sleeping in late, hard drinking, and general laziness, he was still her buddy. Savannah needed his help now, too, and didn't have other options since Troy wouldn't brush a cow or lift a bucket if he had a gun to his head. Though the three of them had shown against each other in 4-H, Troy really believed livestock and anything to do with raising them was far beneath him. For a while, Savannah held on to the belief that he'd come around and enjoy the life she truly loved, but that notion was wrong. He'd shown his true colors; Troy expected to be the first in line for a check when some developer turned Morgan Cattle Company into a bunch of cheesy mini horse farms.

The thought of filing for divorce made her feel like a failure.

She should have stood up for herself and never gotten married.

Savannah watched Eddie emerge from show barn with two buckets of feed filled sloppily over capacity. As he walked, the expensive mix spilled over the edges in clumps. There were little piles of spilled feed everywhere in the lot; he'd been meaning to rake it up, but hadn't gotten around to it yet.

"Hey, Eddie," Savannah called out as she neared the back gate that gave on to the show heifers lot. Rory, seeing all was well ducked through the slats and greeted Eddie with a sniff.

"Oh, Savvy, hey!" Eddie began, now conscious of his careless handling and the fact that he'd mixed the wrong ration for the last several days. He'd meant to feed the proper mix, but he just hadn't gotten around to it. "Sorry about the feed, I'll get that," he added, wobbling toward the bunk. Eddie had an odd, duck like gait; he walked more like an aching old man than a 25-year-old.

"Oh, that's fine," Savannah said, trying not to grimace. "Have you fed Tiara yet?" she asked knowing he'd barely gotten started.

"No-hey I didn't expect you here. Is everything alright?" he asked, but Savannah had faded into the shadows of the barn.

I'll just have to work harder. Savannah thought. *Eddie's good help, and I need him, so I'll be patient.*

Aside from his herdsman failings, being short, bald, and pudgy at 25 didn't make Eddie Quiggly exactly handsome, either. She knew he had always had a crush on her and if there was ever a time to use that power, it was now. Convincing him to do more farm labor would take all of the charm she had. Unlimited free beer and decent wages just might not be enough. Eddie *really* didn't like to work.

Growing up neighbors, Savannah had known Eddie her entire life. Troy also went to their high school but grew up in town. His road to cow showing had come through the charity of Jessica Morgan who'd known Troy's mom and frankly felt sorry for her. Troy's dad was a known philanderer and wandered in and out of his son's life. He suffered from alcoholism and never made solid financial choices, leaving Troy's mother perennially bereft. So, Jessica thought having the adolescent Troy help on the farm would be good for him. Eventually, Troy just became a fixture around the Morgan place and for several years in a row, Harlan even gave him a steer to show at the county fair, again at Jessica's urging. Troy's steers brought big money every year at the auction - Troy took credit for it - but it was only because Jessica charmed the bank President. The bank even donated the steer back to the family so they'd have freezer beef each winter; Jessica had seen to that, too.

While Eddie and Troy spent years together, the two often quarreled and eventually Eddie told Savannah that they couldn't trust him when Eddie caught Troy stealing. When Savannah found out, Troy begged her not to tell; feeling sorry for him, she didn't. After graduation, Savannah went to college, Troy went to trade school, and Eddie stayed around home. One spring break Troy was supposed to be putting out hay, but instead he was horsing around on the tractor, attempting to hot-rod it "Footloose" style. He'd wrecked the tractor and wound up in the hospital. Seeing an opportunity, he threatened to sue Morgan Cattle Company, but when Savannah agreed to marry him, he dropped it. She was only twenty.

The day they announced they were getting married was the worst in Eddie's life. He spent their wedding day getting drunk and wondering why Savannah Morgan had settled.

Savannah filled a bucket with mixed feed and beet pulp for filler, then added mineral, extra protein pellets, a handful of ShowPoof (a hair-enhancing product for the heifers), and grabbed a couple of flakes of alfalfa to finish off the ration. Stepping back into the full sunlight, she wished briefly that she'd grabbed her shades off the kitchen table. There wouldn't be many pretty days like this left.

What if Eddie says no? Who else can I call to get me through the North American Show? Savannah steeled herself again. *He won't say no to me, I'll make sure of it.*

She reached Tiara's pen and before she could pull the spring gate back to allow herself access to the feed bunk, the big russet and white Hereford was already helping herself to the hay that cascaded over Savannah's arm. Nudging her enormous head backwards, she balked, only interested in her meal, not Savannah's need to get it through the gate.

Savannah laughed. "Back up, Big Girl, you either let me in, or you don't get all this," she said gently shoving the 1,600 pound female to get by. Tiara had been in the show barn for over two years and Savannah had worked with the heifer since the day she was born.

"I don't know why you put up with that snide, she's such a damn Primadonna," quipped Eddie as he walked up and set his empty buckets down outside the heifer's pen. "You've got more patience with these rips - you and your Dad-" Eddie remarked then looked away and emitted a nervous breath that reeked of whiskey.

Savannah seized the uncomfortable moment to play on Eddie's vulnerability. She stroked Tiara's head, though the preoccupied heifer never acknowledged the attention.

"It's okay, Eddie. I want to talk about him," she said, then turning away she forced a mist into her eyes while the wind blew a few wayward tresses of hair against her cheek. "I just wish he hadn't left me in such a bind, Eddie."

"What do you mean?"

"Oh, Eddie, there's so much to do now! I've got to get Tiara shown at Louisville and then all these other heifers need broke for the Denver yards sale by January!" she said gesturing toward the pen of 10 feasting bovine in the trap next to Tiara. "I've got to have help! I can't get them all prepped, clipped out, fit for the show, and sold by myself! What am I going to do?" she asked imploringly, her blue eyes opaque from unshed tears.

Eddie hated to see her sad and without meaning to he said a rather uncharacteristic thing. "It's pretty slow at the lumber yard so I'll be laid off soon anyway. I could come over a couple of hours a day and help you break the heifers, if you want."

Savannah was almost appalled at her good fortune.

I must look as pathetic as I feel!

"Eddie, I'd deeply appreciate it, but I'll need help at the show, too. You'll have to come with me, you know. I'll pay your day-wage-whatever amount you want-but someone's got to be there all week at the show and you know Troy won't lift a finger," Savannah said and for added affect she reached out and grabbed Eddie's free hand.

Eddie's heart jumped slightly at Savannah's touch.

What the hell am I thinking, being her damn doormat!

Eddie hated cow shows. Sure, there was lots of fun to be had and beer to be drunk, but that entertainment was always tempered by days filled with work in a stinking barn nursing daily hangovers. Still, Savannah looked so damn *beautiful...*

"Quiggly! Get your greasy hands off my wife!" exclaimed Troy as he briskly strode toward the barn. He had arrived looking for the fight Savannah knew was coming.

Savannah cast a scowl at Rory. "You're going to have to learn to bark when that jerk shows up, you know that!" The dog look chastised, but held his position at her side. "Eddie, thank you SO MUCH, Sweetie. There's going to be fight between Troy and I and it's going to start now. You'd better leave; I'm getting ready to ask him for a divorce," she said hurriedly as she picked up the buckets and headed for the barn.

A stunned Eddie stood speechless as his hand absently reached for the spot where she'd gripped him.

Maybe there was reason to hang around the Morgan place after all.

Troy met him at the gate with a sneer. "We won't be needing your help anymore, but thanks anyway," he said, as usual acting superior.

Eddie scoffed and didn't look back as he headed for the truck. "Actually, Howell, I just hired on." Stepping up into his truck and revving the engine he added with a laugh, "Good luck, old Buddy-you're gonna need it!"

Troy careened into the old barn after Savannah, but his eyes weren't adjusted to the shadowy darkness and he stumbled across a couple of buckets, sending them crashing into a wall. He hated the smell of barn, the mix of dry hay, grain chaff, damp bark used for bedding and old urine from the cattle or some kind of varmint. Troy could see light from the other end of the barn now and make out the feed bags, fence posts, halters and other gear near the entry way. He hated the sight of cattle, always had.

"Why in the hell isn't there a light in here!" he cursed fumbling around for a switch. "Savannah! Where are you? What is Quiggly talking about 'good luck' and 'hiring on'?"

Suddenly, Rory burst from around the corner with a low growl. "Hey! Hey! Dog! What the hell are you growling at me for?" Troy was trying to remain unperturbed, but his heart was beating faster from fright. Recovering his nerve, he reached out and roughly grabbed Savannah's arm. "What's going on with you?" He wanted to rage, but Rory again jumped forward with a growl.

Troy shrank back, instinctively releasing her wrist. "What is with your dog?"

"I know you're itching for a fight, Troy. Let's go in the house to talk," she said striding past. "Be sure to lock the gate."

Cussing under his breath, he carelessly tried to latch the gate, but in his haste it took three fumbled attempts to get it. "If this place wasn't potentially worth so much, I'd tell you to get bent!" he yelled aloud, but Savannah didn't hear his remark, she was already inside the mudroom pulling off her boots.

Savannah went into the office and poured drinks from the side bar into etched highball glasses. "Little early for whiskey, isn't it, my dear?" Troy began, starting off with a dig and desperate to gain the upper hand.

Savannah set his cocktail of whiskey, ice, and cola on one side of her father's massive cherry and cowhide-covered desk. She seated herself on the other side of the formative structure as much to make a point to Troy as to herself. The house smelled sickeningly sweet of the wilting funeral flowers that adorned the front room, hallway, and kitchen. Impulsively, Savannah flicked on the ceiling fan.

"Nice, nice," he mocked, tasting the whiskey and grimacing. Savannah always took her drinks too strong. "Love the way we're 'meeting' in your father's office, Savannah. As if you're in charge."

"Well, starting now, this *is* my office. I quit my job yesterday."

Troy choked as his eyes rolled back in his head. Savannah's excellent wages were keeping them afloat. His latest job selling used trucks at the Dodge dealership had been a little light on commission. "What did you say?" he managed. "Are you going mad from grief or something? We can get you anti-depressants, but you've got to call and get that job back."

Savannah glanced at the office's rustic furnishings. The walls were papered with an old paisley print reminiscent of something out of the 1940's-it had probably hung there that long. Her mother, never one for nostalgia, threatened to repaper the room on numerous occasions, but finally she left Harlan and his outdated décor alone. It was his domain and she stayed out of it, especially after she essentially moved to an apartment in Indianapolis.

The walls were covered with framed prints of stock show champions and favorite heifers and bulls dating back to Savannah's great-grandfather. There were pictures of her show career, too, from peewee showmanship to her first time on green shavings. Images of their top cow family, the Tiara lineage, lined the walls from all the big stocks shows: Denver, Chicago, Ft. Worth, Kansas City, Louisville, Reno, and her father's favorite-Cow Palace in San Francisco. Emboldened by the heritage that surrounded her, Savannah charged on.

"Troy, I want a divorce," she said, her eyes cold and flat without a trace of emotion to soften the blow of her pronouncement.

He didn't take her seriously; it was the job that seriously mattered to him. "Savvy, don't be ridiculous, you and I have been together since we were kids, now back to this job deal –"

"Troy Howell, I *am* serious!" Savannah yelled, immediately irritated by his lack of regard for her opinion. His attitude was just one item in the laundry list of things she didn't like about him. "You and I are through. I am staying on the farm. I'll move out my stuff while you're at work and call Mr. Madsen to file so we can put this whole thing behind us. Our marriage is a farce!"

"You're such a little bitch, Savannah! You planned this with that attorney to keep me from selling this place!"

"You couldn't convince me to walk across the street with you Troy, you're a sniveling wimp and you make me ill-you have for years- and I want out!"

Troy laughed and tried a different approach. "Well, Savvy, as I recall in high school you weren't so hard to convince!"

Savannah was stung by his remark. She was no loose woman and they both knew it. The fact that he'd try to use inaccurate insults to intimidate her was infuriating. Savannah took a long draw of her whiskey and looked up into the smug grin and faded grey eyes of her husband. How she despised his self-serving guts. Without thinking, she flung the whiskey, glass and all, right at him. Troy ducked to avoid the blow, but a syrupy stain the color of tobacco juice slid down the wall of photos as the highball shattered on the hardwood.

"You're a crazy skank, too!" Troy yelled as he jumped from the leather chair and wiped the whiskey from his temple and cheek. He had dropped his glass into his lap and the liquid now sagged the front of his khakis. "If you want a divorce-that's the last thing I'll give you-you're probably already sleeping around on me anyway!"

"Get out, Troy before I don't miss with the next one," Savannah seethed, advancing toward him with the glass he had deposited in his former seat.

Something in Savannah's slow, methodical demeanor in the face of the crude insults he'd flung frightened Troy and he stumbled back, trying to act as if leaving were his original notion.

Savannah Morgan had a wild streak and he wasn't man enough to handle it.

"I'll leave now, but this isn't over."

"Oh, it's over, it's been over since the day you guilt-tripped me into marrying you. But I won't be a fool anymore," Savannah said flatly. She followed him to the back door and stood, unmoving, as she watched him climb into his loaner from the dealership and speed high school-like down the narrow blacktop.

She pulled her cell from her jacket pocket and dialed Madsen's office. She was immediately put through. No, no, problem at all, he'd said. In fact, he'd be happy to prioritize it.

Troy would be served divorce papers by the next afternoon.

~ THREE ~

A Weekend Cowgirl No More

Savannah stood trembling in the doorway as her chest heaved and fell like a lathered horse. She had pushed the situation into a fight. Sure, Troy had come looking for it, but she had made good on his intentions with her show of sitting at her Dad's desk and giving into anger. In recent years she'd become so apathetic about him that she'd ceased bothering to fight, though his snide comments peppered their every conversation. It was her fault that asking Troy for a divorce had turned into a violent event. She was disgusted with herself.

Turning into the house, she paused at the kitchen sink and splashed water on her face then returned to the study. Knowing there was no sense in it, she grabbed a new highball glass from the credenza and poured it half full. She needed fortification to tackle the paperwork and bills on the desk. After an hour of browsing through the stack, Savannah was overwhelmed. Reaching for a drink and then a piece of scratch paper, Savannah made a list of all she needed to do: go to the bank and find out what there was for cash and the balance of her father's operating loan; call the feed company to find out what her dad's ration was and when they delivered it; and call the brokerage firm and her own former company (if her boss's secretary would speak with her) and change the vehicle insurance policies over.

An hour and a glass and a half of Crown Royal later, Savannah felt like she knew less about her financial situation than when she started. She stood, taking the bottle with her to the porch. For the second time in two days, Savannah was sitting outside with a glass of whiskey.

What now?

The thought kept replaying in her increasingly cloudy mind. She pondered the question for a while as Rory joined her. She wished that she'd thought to bring gloves, but she lacked the energy to get up.

Sometime had passed when Rory's ear perked up at the sound of an approaching vehicle. Instantly, Savannah assumed that Troy had returned. She was at once relieved and horrified when her mother's car appeared. Rory leapt up to greet Jessica while Savannah scrambled to somehow hide the evidence of her afternoon drinking spree.

"You might as well quit covering up what you're doing, Savvy!" called Jessica Morgan as she reached down to give Rory a short, obligated pet. "You are your Daddy's daughter, no one can accuse you of being anything but tried and true Morgan now," Jessica laughed at the shamed look on Savannah's face. As she strode forward her chestnut hair bounced jauntily in its fresh-from-the-salon-bob. "Pour me a drink. With what we've got to talk about I could use it."

In stunned compliance, Savannah reached for the bottle she'd tried without success to hide behind the leg of porch swing. Her mother abhorred whiskey and was more of a Chardonnay drinker - and not California either- she'd rather have Chablis any day of the week. For her to drink warm whiskey was a thought unto itself.

Jessica cupped her child's face, affectionately stroking it for a moment, then eased the tumbler from Savannah's grasp as she sat herself gracefully on the porch swing. Without saying a word she sipped, grimaced, then sipped again. Her eyes stared west. Savannah began to cry.

Jessica and her daughter were not particularly close, but they shared some things in common; a love of wine for one - though Savannah attributed most of that to the education on 'cultured things' that her mother had insisted upon. They also both possessed a sharp wit and an excellent proclivity for the English language. Both loved to read, and to write, though Savannah had not written an article that wasn't an insurance report in more than three years. Jessica had always wanted to publish a novel, but she had ditched that notion as her career bloomed in Indianapolis. Looking at them, one could mistake the two for sisters. Jessica was also tall and the elder woman still looked about 35 though she was just under 50, a fact Savannah was proud of and a fact Jessica said was simply a requirement of being a woman in business. She worked at her looks pretty hard.

Savannah wondered how her parents ever came together-they were so different and often at such opposing viewpoints. Harlan tended to rage when he wasn't happy while Jessica was cool and aloof. He wasn't materialistic and didn't worry about things like culture and education. He worked hard every day but his views on cattle and showing were stubbornly antiquated while Jessica was progressive in her career and loved all things modern and sleek. She made the money and supported Harlan's 'cattle habit' as she called it. They both loved life, though, and perhaps, Savannah rationalized, that was the only time her parents fit each other - when they had fun. The elder Morgan's had always seemed like friends when they got along, but never lovers. By the time Savannah was in high school, they had separate bedrooms. When Savannah married Troy, Jessica took an apartment downtown and they had been effectively separated ever since.

Jessica knew her daughter was expecting her to begin, but she wasn't sure where to start. Maybe it was too soon to tell her daughter about all the secrets that the years held, maybe now when everything was askew was the perfect time, she just wasn't sure. So, for a while she sat, her trim figure ensconced perfectly in a brown moleskin pant suit and matching high-heeled boots.

Finally, Jessica spoke, annoyed with herself that she didn't have the courage to tell all, but knowing that she just wasn't ready. "Well, babe, I'm heading up to Chicago this afternoon. I've got a job offer at a big firm up there and I'll probably take it. I hope you'll understand; I just can't stay here with your Daddy gone." Jessica sipped the whiskey again.

"Mom, I know you're leaving," Savannah responded evenly.

The older woman touched Savannah's shoulder. "You're more mature than I gave you credit for, Savannah, and you don't need me. This place has always been yours anyway."

"I wish we could have figured out a way to get along and do more together."

"I do, too. But, your Dad's personality, was, you know, well, he could be difficult," Jessica said plainly. Both women knew what she meant. "I'm glad you talked to Roland about the will yesterday."

Savannah didn't want to relive the scene in Mr. Madsen's office, but she had to tell Jessica about her other legal plans. "I asked, no, I told Troy I was divorcing him today, Mom. It got pretty ugly, but it's always like that with him."

"Yes, Roland said that you called. I'm so glad you did," she said, then added with a small smile. "You dad would be overjoyed!"

Savannah exhaled loudly, she felt nothing but tired. "I should have never married him, Mom."

"No, Babe you shouldn't have. And, I should have tried harder to stop you, but-" her voice trailed off, she had so many regrets. "Well, if you need me, I'm a phone call away. I know it will be tough to figure out what to do with this place. God knows your Dad probably left the finances a mess. But, see what you can do and if you decide you don't want this place, we'll sell it."

Savannah stiffened, lifting her chin with resolve. "I'm not selling it, Mom. I want-no- I - will make it work."

"Absolutely, if its what you want, that's fine, Savannah," Jessica said, rising. "I need to get going, I'm on my way to the airport right now. I'll be home around Christmas or maybe you could just come up and see the city- oh, no-of course not, you'll have chores and Denver cattle to get ready, I know," her mother added with a sigh that expressed all the times she'd been displaced because of shows and chores over the years. She stood and embraced Savannah, who struggled slightly to get up.

Jessica stepped off the porch and walked to her car. Before getting inside she paused. "Savannah, just in case you're considering it, don't stay home from Louisville. You go to that show! You and your Dad may not have gotten along, but showing is what you both loved."

Morning arrived for Savannah complete with a slamming headache and a case of dry-mouth that would have stopped traffic had she breathed on anyone. Trying desperately not to aggravate the pounding in her head, Savannah rolled over to look out the window and check the alarm clock: 7:30 am. Not bad for the night I had, Savannah rationalized.

Now if I can get up without puking...

Swinging her slender legs around she realized one sock was three-quarters off of her foot, the other was lost and she had slept in under-wear and a half unbuttoned blouse. Her bra gouged her back and shoulder where she'd lain on the contraption all night. Her jeans and work shoes were wadded up in a corner amid a little pile of dried mud and manure scattered on the hardwood. Savannah scowled at the mess she'd no doubt tracked through the entire house. Sitting up, she swooned from the hangover and had to lean against the bedpost. She felt horrible, but there were hungry mouths to feed outside and she needed a drink of water something awful.

Downstairs and dressed as Savannah prepared coffee and drank the much-needed water she heard Eddie pull in.

"Thank God you're here, Eddie," Savannah began. "Help yourself to some coffee."

Eddie eyed her closely. "You alright?"

"Yeah, just a bit hung-over. Things didn't go real smooth with Troy, mom came by, and I, well, I think I drank an entire bottle of Crown Royal by myself," Savannah said, shaking her head at the realization that the only glass she'd wasted had been the one she'd thrown at Troy's face. She glanced toward the entrance to the office.

There's another mess to clean up today, she thought, wishing her head didn't hurt so badly.

Eddie didn't know what to say about Savannah and Troy's situation. Comforting wasn't his thing. "I can stay and clip a few this morning and afternoon if you want."

"That's good. I'll do chores and you can sharpen your clipper blades."

"Don't you want some breakfast?" Eddie asked with a grin as he pressed the lid on his portable coffee mug.

Savannah's eyes widened and she shook her head delicately as she reached back to capture her blonde hair in a ponytail holder. "Eddie, I can't eat a thing right how, but let's eat lunch at Billie's bar - I may want to hit it again by then!"

"I doubt that!"

———— • ◆ • ————

Outside, Savannah and Rory headed to the barn to chore while Eddie went towards the workshop and the grinding wheel. He had brought along his 71-12's, an antiquated set of clippers used by the old-school types to really shear some hair. He needed to sharpen the blades on his Andi's, too. The Andi's he preferred since they were a much smaller, lighter set of shears that clipped away much less hair at a time. The 71-12's impressed people because the older, famous cow clippers could wield the ghastly blades with ease. While he hated the heavy things, Eddie was not a famous cattle fitter and was too cheap to buy an updated set of Andi's.

Through the morning and afternoon, Savannah worked with more vigor than Eddie could have managed on his best day. Though they were prepping for the Louisville show, the Denver pen heifers needed work, too. Harlan tended to cut it close on getting sale heifers ready and Savannah always thought they looked too skinny at Denver; she planned to have them in better shape and be more than just green broke, too. Savannah didn't even know which calves would be good enough to make the sale so she and Eddie decided to give them a more critical appraisal after he sheared off some baby hair. They ran sets of two at a time into the holding pens behind the large working chute. One by one, each calf went into the chute to be washed then blown out. Once dry and brushed, Savannah worked to keep the young calves calm by gently rubbing the bellies or necks with a show-stick while Eddie sheared on their freshly dried hair. He ran the clippers over their heads, necks, and top lines and worked to make shoulders look smoother and hips appear wider. He opened the bottom door of the aluminum chute and risked being kicked a time or two to clip their bellies and the backs of their hocks. Russet and white hair fell all around the chute, the tuffs floating around and settling like a thick carpet that looked as though they had laid down a hide rug. Shearing off the old hair was a time consuming task, but by lunchtime, Savannah was happy with their handiwork.

"These really look nice blocked out, don't you think?" She handed Eddie a beer from the fridge inside the barn.

Eddie accepted his drink. Standing, his knees popped and snapped. "Damn it working cattle makes you get old," he swore. Too late he realized that he should have brought along kneepads. Sipping the beer, he reached up with his left hand and pushed the ball cap back to reveal his baldhead. With the back of his forearm he wiped away the beads of sweat.

"They're coming along, I guess. We'll see how they look when you load the trailer for Denver."

"Hey-let's go over to Billie's and grab a late lunch-I'm finally hungry!"

"I thought you'd never ask!"

———————————•◆•———————————

The vet's office was a 45-minute drive. It was about the last way Savannah wanted to start the morning, but several of the Denver sale heifers needed surgically dehorned and with Louisville and the holiday's coming up, there wasn't much time before the old vet left to winter in Florida. The new vet at the clinic was nice, but Harlan thought the last job he'd done was careless and not aesthetic enough; the heifer's heads had to look pretty to sell high.

Stepping out of the house, Savannah's body was unprepared for the shock of the cold morning. As the wind whipped at her slightly damp hair, she thought with chagrin about how her father was used to getting up early while she'd become soft in her years as a 'weekend cowgirl', one of the many terms Troy used to mock her. She vowed to get on a schedule of rising early and working hard all day. At the barn, the calves hadn't yet come up for feed. The ground crunched lightly as the frost gave way under Savannah's boots and the aluminum pipe gates glittered under the security lamp above the barn, the metal cold to the touch as Savannah pushed through and hollered at the calves.

"Hoo-Who-woo, Who-Woo! Come on, girls, Com'on!" Savannah called as she entered the barn and began clamoring around for feed. By the time she'd lugged around 50-pound bags of pre-mixed show feed, filled three buckets, and hauled them to the bunks, the calves were just meandering up to investigate. Rory stood on guard to muster along any stragglers, but Savannah patted him and told him to sit. "You'll get your chance to help me this morning, I promise!"

Savannah opened the main gate out wide and walked up to the truck and trailer. Without preamble, Rory leapt into the bed and ran excitedly from side to side ready to go. Savannah started the truck and backed down toward the calf traps, being as careful as she could not to scrape the sides of the gate in the tight fit. It took five tries to line the trailer up decently with the heifer's pens and even then it wasn't the greatest, but the first milestone had been accomplished. "If I ever have a daughter, she is going to learn to back up a truck and trailer!" Savannah mused aloud.

After the calves had spent 15 or so minutes eating, Savannah and Rory moved into the pen and began herding them toward the open trailer door that she'd swung across the entrance to their trap. The calves moved up fine but balked at jumping on. Having never loaded a trailer, much less left the farm, they kept doubling back, but the dog nipped and growled enough the discourage much flight. Finally, with persistence she didn't know she had, Savannah shoved the first calf up into the trailer and the rest quickly followed. She hustled to slam the door shut and lock it. "Part Two, Accomplished!" she exclaimed as she drove out of the driveway.

Savannah had driven a loaded rig before, but it was always with her dad and always around home. Fortunately, Eddie had helped her hook up the night before. Once she got started, everything was basically the same as driving a car, of course, it was just that she knew she lacked experience, especially if she had to back around somewhere. Her vet's office was a straight-in, straight-out shot, so everything was going to go okay.

Once there, she guided the vet on her opinion on the horns, a job she never liked, but needed to be done. For the show, cattle needed to look cosmetically done, so achieving a smooth, polled-looking head was the goal. The vet always asked for the owner's opinion on the job, and even though the calves were under anesthesia, Savannah always got a little squeamish. But as Troy's 'weekend cowgirl' taunts came to mind again, she pushed aside her weakness. "Take that side down a bit sharper, Doc," Savannah said with renewed intent.

When Savannah had the groggy calves loaded and the vet paid she felt sure she was nearly home free, but someone with a horse trailer had completely double-parked her truck.

"Hey, Doc, can you get this trailer moved?" she asked.

"Already tried. Owner's got the keys with him and they're in the middle of a horse C-section. We can't go in the room unsterilized. Just back around," he said, returning to his washing up.

Savannah felt a small twinge of panic rise up in her throat.

Freakin' rude horse jocks!

"I, I, well, I'm not the best at 'backing around' you might say. I apologize, but maybe you could give me a hand?"

The old vet looked irritated at her perfunctory request. "Get in your truck and I'll guide you around, Missy," he remarked, already assuming a position around the side of her truck.

Savannah was chagrined but couldn't refuse the help. She was hoping he'd just volunteer to back it for her, but that obviously wasn't going to happen.

*Please just let me get this thing out of here without doing anything stupid.*Savannah silently prayed, realizing even God must think it was ridiculous that she couldn't maneuver her truck and trailer.

She backed around, her eyes alternating between the side of the vet clinic and the erratic arm movements and yells of the vet as he supposedly helped. Frankly, she couldn't understand a damn bit of what he was trying to do. He acted like she ought to be able to interpret which way to cut the wheel just from some unknown arm signal. Perhaps his movements were some kind of man thing-she certainly couldn't decipher them! Savannah hadn't thought since kindergarten square dancing lessons that she didn't know her right arm from her left. Finally, she was nearly around the building when she heard a loud 'thud'!

Uh-oh.

She could see the old vet scurrying over to the building just in time to see that she'd nailed it.

"You hit the damn broadside of a barn!" He yelled. "How in the hell did 'ya do that?"

Savannah was embarrassed but also sick of the old doc's lack of patience. "I'm so sorry, Doc, I just didn't see it!"

She actually started cracking up as she pulled out onto the road.

• ◆ •

She and Eddie spent the daylight hours in a routine of working on the show stock. Since Tiara had been left standing in Kansas City, Louisville was her second to last chance at winning one of the big three majors. Savannah intended to go and win.

Now, just days away from heading into the show, Tiara looked nice, but keeping the whites bright on a Hereford coming in from a muddy barn lot was a job. It seemed like she bought bluing every other day.

It was beginning to feel like farm life was running rather smoothly until the morning Savannah realized that she hadn't put out for the cows in days. For the first time in a week she felt shame and embarrassment at her inept management – Harlan would have *never* let the mama cows run clean out of hay! She couldn't believe they hadn't broken through the hot wire fence to get to the other round bales. Chagrined, Savannah dialed Eddie on her cell.

"Hey, we forgot to put out hay last night and the girls are totally out," she said when Eddie answered in a groggy voice. "Could you come over now and help me?"

Eddie was not one to rise early, not even for Savannah. "Can't that wait, its 6:30 in the morning!"

"No, the cows'll be into the round bales by the time you usually get here!"

"Well, just shut the gate on those snides then and wait! Can't you do a damn thing without a man?" Eddie growled, instantly sorry he'd been cross with her, but he'd planned on sleeping another two hours.

Savannah was stung by the truth in Eddie's remarks.

Am I really helpless without a man?

~ FOUR ~

A Proposition

Savannah's evenings had become the best part of the day. Instead of feeling lonely, she felt free and relaxed. Besides, she was exhausted. Sometimes Eddie stayed for dinner and a few beers, other times not. Savannah didn't mind his company, though for a 25-year-old he could get grouchy awfully fast. Many evenings she enjoyed a hot bath and tonight's was accompanied by a glass of pinot noir. As she inhaled the scent of lavender essential oil that she'd added to the water, her mind turned to thoughts of the upcoming show. Leaning back and taking a drink she decided that she was going to have fun in Louisville! Cattle shows and the friends from around the country were something she looked forward to all year. It was getting to be the season, too, with Louisville coming up and then the National Western in Denver approaching in early January.

Savannah's plans were interrupted by Rory's sharp bark. Since she was staying alone at the farm, she'd taken to letting the dog sleep in the foyer. The dog's bark became a low growl as Savannah heard the front door lock turn in the jam and the seal give way, letting someone in.

"Quit your frickin' yippin'!" Savannah heard Troy yelling. "Savannah where the hell are you? Come get this mutt of yours off my frickin' leg! Damn it! Back off dog!" he yelled, clearly afraid.

Savannah didn't take time to dry off and grabbed a heavy fleece robe for cover. *What is Troy doing here at 11:00 at night?*

He sounded drunk.

Descending the stairs, her fear was confirmed, Troy was sloppy drunk and standing in the pool of mud he'd tracked all over her front hall.

"How'd you get in here?"

"Will you call off this damn dog?" Troy was practically screaming. "Your dad certainly made it hard to find the key! I had to get soaking wet hunting around the flower bed," Troy complained loudly. Slurring his words, he clumsily tried to remove his long over coat. Suddenly, he turned to look at Savannah for the first time. "Well, well, look at you. Probably not even wearing any underwear I'll bet and just showered up. You gotta boyfriend comin' over?" Troy's eyes barely focused. He was slinging the old, unfounded insults once again.

Classic, despicable, Troy.

"Get out, Troy, you're drunk. I take it you received my divorce papers?"

"Yeah, real nice the way you sent them to work and I had to sign for them right in front of everybody like a jackass! You coulda told me, at least," Troy whined, starting to advance toward her. Savannah realized she should have changed the locks.

"I did tell you I wanted a divorce, several times, actually. Anyway, when I said get out, I mean it. If you want to talk about this, call Mr. Madsen."

"*Call Mr. Madsen,*" he mocked. "Who do you think you are to deny me? I'm you're husband!" Troy tried to make a run at her and lunged up the stairwell. Instead, he fell forward, hitting his face on the hardwood step. Savannah wasn't sure whether to help him or let him lie. She had an overwhelming urge to erase him from her life.

Troy looked up, dazed, and surprised Savannah by crying, actually weeping profusely. "Savannah, you can't leave me, you gotta to stay with me! I need the money, it's serious! Tonight they said they'll kill me..."

"What are you talking about? Who?" Savannah was incredulous as she gingerly approached the pathetic looking heap on the floor. His lip was split as was his brow bone. Blood trickled down into his eye and his teeth were stained red from his bleeding lip. Troy slobbered and tried to sit up.

"Savannah, I've got to talk to you, please just let me talk, okay?" He looked utterly terrified. Savannah sat down a few steps above him.

"What's going on?"

"I'm in a little bit of trouble, well, okay, a whole lot of trouble. I've been doing a little playing out at the track, I mean just occasionally. When I spent through our money, well, then I had to do a little borrowing. I borrowed against our house – I know! I know! Don't be pissed, okay!" He yelled, clutching his head. "And, that was really going good, ya know? But well, then I listened to a guy who just didn't know his picks worth a crap and well, ya know, then when that went wrong, I didn't have the money to back up the bets so I had to get a little help."

"Where'd you get the money, Troy?" Savannah said evenly not wanting to know the answer. He'd already admitted to leveraging all the equity in their home and using all of their savings. She had spent so much time ignoring him that she had no idea what a fool she had been.

"There's a couple of guys out at the track that helped me a bit, I mean they offered just to loan me the money for a while, but that was before your Dad died and I haven't been on a real good streak lately, so they're wanting to get paid back-"

"You borrowed from a loan shark? You've got to be joking! How were you going to pay them back if you've already tried to break us?" Savannah put her head in her hands, she didn't want any part of Troy Howell's debts. She had to call Madsen in the morning and figure out if she was liable for the misdeeds of her idiot spouse.

Troy looked up and spoke again, this time feigning niceness. "Well, see Savannah, that's just it. Don't get mad or anything, but with your Daddy dying when he did, that just paved the way for you and I to get out of this mess. We can borrow against this place-its been paid for forever-there's got to be a ton of equity-" Savannah cut him off, Troy was a sniveling rat. Standing up she kicked at him with her bare foot.

"Get out now, you pathetic excuse for a man!"

Troy stood up, wiping his sleeve against his bloody lip and leaning on the railing for support, his demeanor instantly flaming from pathetic to furious. "I'm not leaving until we work this out, Savannah! All you've got to do is convince your mom we need a little cash!"

"Get out!"

Troy attempted to hold his ground. "Hey! I've come clean about this little issue, so now you know what I need. I need cash and you can access it. It's not like you even have to sell this dump!"

Savannah's patience snapped at his constant reference to 'their' problem. His gambling was something she hadn't even known about. It was not her problem!

"If you think you'll get one cent of Morgan money to feed your disgusting habit, you've got another thing coming. Get off my land, Troy Howell or I'll call the police!" Savannah exclaimed, turning away, but Troy lunged for her. He grabbed her around the neck and flung her to the floor, attempting to choke her.

"Shut up! Shut up! I will get the money!" Troy screamed and temporarily overpowered Savannah as he lumbered on top of her. Suddenly, he fell back with a shriek of pain. Rory was at his neck growling fiercely and biting. Savannah let him get bit as she grabbed at her neck and tried to breathe. Struggling upright, she ran five steps to the hall closet and pulled the shotgun from behind the rack of winter coats. Rory bit at the drunken man as he screamed and scrambled toward the front door. Savannah ran to the kitchen to dial 911. He made it to porch then limped to his black

SUV. Throwing it reverse, he careened out of the driveway, knocking her mailbox off the post as he went. Wielding the gun on one hip, Savannah watched him go as she shivered, half wet and nearly choked in the cold night air. Into the receiver she addressed the 911 dispatcher:

"I want to report a drunk driver last seen heading south on the Morgan Road."

—————————— •◆• ——————————

Savannah wasted no time in serving Troy with a restraining order the next morning, one that he had the pleasure of being served while still in jail from the drunk driving charge he'd received the night before. He knew Savannah must have called him in since two cop cars were basically waiting for him only a few miles from the farm. He had cursed her, fought, and acted the fool, causing him to also get slapped with a resisting arrest charge. He couldn't get bailed out for at least twelve hours due to the DWI, but even then he wasn't even sure whom he'd call. After he'd calmed down and started to sober up, he'd had the rest of the night to think about how to get even with Savannah for the continual hell she was putting him through. She was serious about divorce, a thought that terrified him, but he needed cash and a second mortgage on the farm was about the best idea he had come up with. There was one advantage to staying in jail-at least he wouldn't get beat up again by the guys from the track - but jail was no solution. There had to be a way to force Savannah into staying married to him or at least find a plausible way for her to have to pay him to leave. Suddenly, Troy jumped up and clapped his hands.

"Eddie!" he said aloud, awakening another drunk who rolled over and flipped him off.

Fifteen minutes later the guard opened the door. "Howell!" bellowed the man in uniform. "Get out here, Inmate, you're released. Is there someone you'd like to call for a ride?"

"What about my SUV?"

"Your car has been impounded, Inmate, since you couldn't make bail. Come up with $2,500 bucks and you get it back. How 'bout that call now?"

———————————— • ◆ • ————————————

I am some kind of sucker to fall for his crap and hers, too.

Eddie watched Troy emerge through the brown metal doors of the county jail. He was unshaven and had a cut above his eye and caked blood on his lip. He carried a thick manila envelope.

"Damn am I glad you were willing to come for me, Quig. Man, I really appreciate it. Hey, you got time to go for a cup of coffee or something? I need t' run an idea past you," Troy said, tossing the envelope in the back seat. "Bitch slapped a restraining order on me and I'm the one who got beat up-would you believe that?"

Eddie just shrugged and drove them to the Roadway Café on the edge of town. He really wished he wasn't in the middle of it. But at least the thought that maybe Savannah had beat Troy up was amusing.

A busty waitress with a heart tattoo above her billowing cleavage served them both coffee and tossed menus in front of them, a move that demonstrated she had more than one tattoo. "Did you see that Quig? Whew! That chick's gotta rack!" Troy sneered and watched the woman waggle away.

"Howell, don't call me Quig. What do you want, anyway, I've got to get out the farm."

"Oh right, so you can help out my wife with her cattle enterprise! That's getting you far in life, Man!" Troy sucked back the contents of his coffee. "You wanna know what she did to me last night-how I ended up in jail? Its her fault, you know!"

"No."

As if Eddie hadn't spoken, Troy continued. "I'll tell you what she did! I went there last night to apologize and she knocked me down the stairs, that's how I got this bruise on my face, not mention my lip. I don't want to divorce her, but I think she's up to something with another man and I'm just gonna have to."

"I don't think you're going to get much choice! And, there's no one else. Don't be an ass."

"Oh, I forgot, you're in love with her," Troy said rudely. Moving on, and as if the two topics were connect he added, "Hey, Ed, you want to make some money? I mean legit cash money?"

"What'r you into now, Howell, drug dealing?"

"Yeah, right no, joke, Ed. I gotta great racket going at the track. Gotta guy that gives me the best picks ever, I'm making money over the moon. I'd like to cut you in on my picks-for a little favor."

"Like what?"

"Well, glad you're interested! " Troy sneered. "Okay, so you and my wife are going to Louisville in a day or two, right?" Eddie nodded. "Well, I just want you to use your eyes and ears - just keep things in perspective - and let me know what she's up to."

"She'll be up to showing cows, you idiot."

Troy scoffed. "Come on, Ed, we all know they'll be plenty of meat heads sniffing around my wife. If Savvy is going to divorce me, I need to be armed with some defenses. Women these days get all the goods and men just get the shaft. I need to know if she's got any, say, lucrative business deals going on or if she's, well, you know, sleepin' around on me."

"You're out of your mind! Savannah's not like that!"

"Yeah - and if she was don't you wish it was with you!"

The blush of truth on Eddie's cheeks made Troy snort coffee. He eased himself closer to Eddie's face, the ripped vinyl booth seat squeaking crudely as he leaned in. "Come one, Ed. Let's be straight, here. My wife is one hot girl. She's tall, leggy, and blonde, with a nice bod and men like the fact that she's friendly. She's going to get lots of attention once everybody finds out she's almost single. All I want to know is what's going on with my property when I'm not around to protect it."

"Howell, you're a rat! I'm not helping you extort money out of Savannah-"

"Oh come on, Ed! You actually think all this helping out is going to get you into her bed someday? Whatever! You're good and reliable, Eddie, and she's always thought of you as a real pal. Good ole' Eddie, she always says, never will deny her of anything she asks for-"

"Shut up and walk home!" Eddie yelled, shoving brusquely away from the booth and stomping into the chilly November morning.

He wasn't taking Howell up on his offer.

~ FIVE ~

Tying In

"Eddie! Wake up! I drove all the way here! I'm so proud of myself," Savannah said, poking at him, the look on her face one of pure joy. She was just pulling off the interstate and into the expo grounds. "I'm really getting a knack for pulling a truck and trailer. Come on! Wake up! We can get in the barn in two hours to make stalls."

Eddie groaned. He was officially on duty, his two-hour nap having done nothing more than make him want to lounge a little longer. He grunted loudly and passed gas as Savannah ground the trailer to an abrupt halt in the tie out area just off the main drive.

Savannah took a deep breath as she looked around. The expo grounds were so familiar to her; she'd seen the big looming barns and show arenas many times in her life, but taking care of things, no, being in charge of the stock, made her view the grounds differently. She had set her truck and trailer in a row among probably another 200 or so such rigs, mostly Ford duallys or F250's that pulled long, shiny aluminum trailers. The huge lot was a hubbub of activity. It was the area that everyone referred to as "tie-outs", or basically where everyone parked their trailers, stored extra tack, and bedded the cattle down at night.

Savannah saw friends leading cattle from afar and gave a big wave. People were pulling in, trying to locate a suitable spot that wouldn't get too muddy and unloading everything from feedbags to tents, metal gates to beer coolers. Up and down the dirt and gravel rows exhibitors were in motion. People were walking stock up to the barns to stall in for the various breed shows and sales, others were blowing out using big generators to pull power and just as many people were simply standing around idly visiting with friends they probably hadn't seen in several months. Impatient calves wearing colorfully halters and even Velcro neck sweats pranced nervously as if also sensing the aura of excitement. Savannah was chilly in the perennially muggy air; it was only 45 degrees, but she'd soon be sweating on account of the humidity and the labor of hauling equipment to the barn. She was going to love every minute of it. Troy was nowhere in sight and she knew Harlan would approve that she'd brought Tiara to try again and win it. This was Louisville! She was going to party and find someone cute to flirt with.

What was the name of that guy who always fit cattle for Rawlings Ranch?

"Hey! Sunshine! You want to give me a hand with your stock and quit your damn daydreamin'?" Eddie barked from inside the trailer as he thrust a bale of straw at her. Savannah laughed as she tossed it outside. "What's so funny? You're just high on life, aren't you?" Eddie remarked sarcastically.

"Eddie, you're grumpy this morning-I think you need a girlfriend!" Savannah said with a straight face. She saw Eddie blush almost purple and she laughed once more.

———— •◆• ————

The day passed so quickly that Savannah hardly realized it was chore time until she saw other people rustling pans and mixing feed. She had spent the last hour talking to two girlfriends in the Shorthorn barn and filling them in on the impending break up with Troy. They were sympathetic to her situation.

"Well, I'd better get back to my stalls and feed. Eddie will be getting mighty pissy, I imagine," Savannah stood up to leave.

Macy Rawlings pulled back her shirtsleeve to reveal a diamond-circled Rolex watch; Macy's husband's family had old land and oil money and ran a big spread West of Oke City. Macy was a blast for a friend-she didn't have to work too hard and was always up for a good time. "Yeah, its 4:30 up here, ya'll. I better go find Stetson and see what he's doing, too," said the brunette as she ran a hand through her spiky haircut. "Hey, where are we all going for dinner? Why don't ya'll join Stetson, me and the crew?" she suggested, casting a coy glance at Savannah and their other friend, Bella Paulsson, the fashionably dressed redhead from North Dakota. Bella smiled; she knew what Macy had in mind.

"Now why would I want to eat dinner with you guys? Eddie keeps me totally entertained," Savannah said, feigning ignorance. The door would be wide-open with the Rawlings' crewman, Tripp Crothers; she'd seen how he'd been looking at her all day.

"Oh, I'm sure having a short, balding, grouchy guy around is damn entertaining, but it sure isn't *satisfying*!" Macy chided, nodding in the direction of Tripp Crothers' rear end as the Texan bent over and afforded the girls a nice view of his tight butt. Tripp wasn't too far away, but the girls knew they couldn't be heard over the noise level in the barn.

"Macy!" Savvy exclaimed, as she allowed herself a longer look at the hunky fitter in starched Cinch jeans.

"You know how you *love* that Texas drawl, Savvy," Bella crooned. "We surely don't want Tripp to be disappointed-its already gotten all over this fairgrounds that you're as good as divorced. You *need* to have some fun. Hey, I'll meet you guys at the bar later."

Savannah paused for a moment and gave both her friends a hug.

"What was that for?" Macy asked, amused.

"I just wanted you to know how fun it is to see you girls. It's going to be a good week, I think," Savannah said, then smiling she added. "Eddie and I will meet your crew in about two hours after we feed and exercise. Cool?"

"Very cool. I'll save a spot next to a certain handsome man just for you," Macy said as she patted Savannah's arm with a perfectly manicured hand that sported a three- carat diamond.

Chore time sounds like work, Savannah thought as she walked back to the stalls, but she knew it was arguably the most interesting time of the day at a cattle show. Amid the constant drone of high-powered fans, familiar smells of molasses, prairie hay, and musky-sweet feedstuffs, circulated around as cowboys and cowgirls watched cattle eat, then get brushed and blown out again and generally shown off. The close of the day was the time to see and be seen. Everyone who was anyone (or who thought they were) was either working on their own cattle or meandering around various stalls to appraise stock.

Because of the constant noise, Savannah thought it seemed like being at the show was like watching a silent movie. The barns were almost always a misty haze of show sheen being sprayed co-mingled with the dust from boots and chaff from hay. On and off went the loud whine of blowers as livestock hair was manicured into a fluffy, shiny sheen like a gorgeous fur coat. Deals were almost always cut at chore time. People discussed purchasing heifers or bulls private treaty or potential buyers came around to look at cattle that would be offered later in an auction ring. Both the seriously analytical and the simply curious perused the cattle saying gossipy thing like: '*That heifer will never get around that other heifer in class*' or '*she's got no shot in hell to beat the such-and-such heifer when they already bought and paid for the judge*' or '*you know what they paid for that female?*' and '*Course, you know outta that dam of hers, she'll never make the tan bark next year 'cause she won't stay sound enough*'.

Show cattle people were an interesting lot, Savannah mused as she watched Eddie guffawing a few steps away with some other guys. At once dear friends and fierce competitors, the talk cow-jocks spread in the barns could often make or break a potential big-dollar deal, the success of a heifer's show career, or a stud bull's semen sales.

Still, nothing gets better than this, Savannah thought as she pulled the scotch comb from her right rear pocket and walked up to brush Tiara's already perfect hair once again.

———————————— •◆• ————————————

"Hey, where are you going? We don't need to stop at the hotel, I'm starving!" Eddie complained as Savannah turned left from the fairgrounds and headed the dually truck into the parking lot of Louisville's matriarch hotel, *The Executive Inn.*

"I'll just be a minute, Eddie. Get a beer and keep the truck running." Savannah grabbed her garment bag before Eddie could protest further. She usually didn't fuss a whole lot about her appearance after a day in the barns, but she usually was married or had her Dad around to make her feel like she should behave. Tonight, she was going to flirt with that hot Texan Tripp Crothers.

Inside the "Exec" as everyone referred to the outdated old hotel, Savannah saw a few friends of her father's and paused to accept more condolences as she had been all day. It was nice to talk to the men she'd seen at his funeral and others she didn't even realize her father had known. Savannah fought tears a few times, but finally got checked in and up to her room. She wasn't going to cry over missing her dad tonight.

The emptying of Savannah's garment bag immediately covered the faded bedspread. With haste she made her way through the mountain of clothes to locate just the right outfit in her 'cow show couture collection' as she liked to call it. Dressing at shows was a marriage of both function (jeans and down vests or pullovers to keep warm) and fashion (big sterling and turquoise cross jewelry, gaudy sparkle belts of leather encased with Swarovski crystals, bright multi-stone rings and bracelets, colorful Ostrich-print cowboy boots, and expensive leather or designer handbags) that kept Western apparel makers doing a brisk business. Savannah wanted to look chick, but not overdone; she couldn't out-do Macy's expensive taste in cowgirl accessories, but she didn't want to look dumpy. She knew she was pretty, but she wanted to be hot!

Pulling the sides of her long blonde hair up and letting a few tendrils cascade around her face, she added a bit more mascara and some black eyeliner along with frosty pink lipstick. She exchanged her stretched out jeans for a starched pair that didn't have manure stains around the cuffs and completed the look with a slinky red top and big, jeweled Concho belt she'd bought in Ft. Worth the winter before. Standing back to eye her appearance, Savannah was satisfied as she added a bit more powder to dampen the slight redness of her cheeks. She looked pretty good and it only took 15 minutes, hardly even enough time to thoroughly annoy Eddie.

At the restaurant, they parted ways at the door as Eddie headed for the bar while Savannah was immediately joined in conversation with Macy about how adorable her new belt was. True to her word, Macy made it work so that Tripp Crothers found a seat right next to Savannah in a rather tight-fitting booth. Savannah wasted no time turning on the charm. She felt like she's been squandering herself for years.

"I hope I'm not taking up too much room over here for you, Tripp," she said, smiling sweetly. She shifted just slightly so that part of her thigh and knee practically overlapped with Tripp's. The starch of their jeans then crunched every time they moved.

"The only thing better than you sitting next to me would be if you were already sitting on my lap," Tripp answered as he winked at her with his broad-set chestnut eyes. Savannah acted offended as Tripp asked her what she was drinking, but Savannah didn't bother to scoot over much.

The evening was off to a fine start as she asked Tripp to order her a Crown and Seven.

The Exec's bar made more money during the two weeks of the livestock show than during any other single event combined for the balance of the year. That the drinks were overpriced and many of the waitress's surly (and homely) didn't seem to matter. At one time the bar had been meant for Southern hospitality and even a bit of luxury, but years of hard-drinking guests clad in boots and muddy shoes had rendered the place tired and worn. The English Tudor style décor in the dank lounge was just old with dark wood and paneling, green and burgundy on the carpets and walls, and the mahogany furniture was gouged and scarred. The place was always completely overcrowded by about 9 pm and remained that way until around 2 am. The hotel management tried to limit the number that entered, but people always snuck past the bouncers or crawled under tables to secure a spot; it was where everyone expected to be seen.

Usually there wasn't a decent seat to be found unless someone you knew got up and left, but Savannah found herself seated comfortably between Tripp Crothers and Macy with Bella leaning up against Macy's chair for a back rest. Tripp was talking to a few guys next to him and she was chatting with her girlfriends, but they were completely aware of each other. Savannah's skin jumped every time Tripp leaned over to say something silly or flirtatious; she wasn't sure what she wanted with Tripp, but she was enjoying the ride!

"Hey, ya'll, I need to check my make-up," Macy said standing up and patting her belly. She obviously needed to use the restroom.

"Me, too. This beer is going right through me!" Bella giggled, shaking her long red hair a bit and setting her beer on Savannah's table.

"First day in always does that to me, too. We're all in such a great mood to see each other that we just party too hard!" Savannah laughed as she started to stand up, but Tripp grabbed her wrist playfully and held her down.

"Hey, Hottie, where you goin'?"

"Save my spot, will you, Tripp?" Savannah wasn't quite finished when Tripp pulled her right into his lap.

"If someone takes your chair, I've got a place you can sit, remember?"

———————— ◆ ————————

"Whew! Tripp is sooooo into you. He's such a major flirt!" Macy exclaimed.

"Girl! You're moving fast! Way to score this one!" Bella chimed in as she removed a bronze-hued gloss from her purse and began to apply it.

Savannah sat down in a heap on the bench provided, her heart slamming. She knew she had only to say the word and she and Tripp would be upstairs. But that wasn't the way she operated.

As if Macy had read Savannah's mind, she sat down next to her, still smiling broadly. "Are you freaked out?" Savannah looked up at her meekly. "Bella, our girl here is freaked out!"

"I'm not freaked out, I'm just not sure I'm ready to let Tripp get his way that easily."

Macy started to add something, but Savannah waved a hand to silence her. "I'm just used to flirting a little and making a few cute remarks, you know? I mean, up until now, everyone knew I was married and that even though Troy was a dork, I was still married and I honored that."

Macy smiled warmly at Savannah and sat down on the ladies' room bench.

"You don't have to do anything you don't want to. You know that, right?"

Savannah was mortified; it was like she was sitting here talking to two racy older sisters. "I'm not even divorced yet-I don't want to be tacky. Besides, its not like I actually am silly enough to want to *date* Tripp..." Savannah said, a sly smile spreading across her face. She glanced in the mirror and was glad for the dark bar so Tripp wouldn't be able to see the patches of scarlet creating blotches up and down her neck. "Does that sound awful?" she asked her two friends.

"No, of course not. This is not our mother's era. Have some fun!" Macy announced, standing to straighten a $1,000 silver and turquoise Concho belt over her Diesel-brand jeans.

"Besides, Tripp's totally branded you as his chick for the week with that little move he pulled in front of everyone," Bella added, a twinge of jealousy in her voice. "If you don't want Tripp, can I flirt with him?"

" I don't care who flirts with him!" Savannah exclaimed in mock exasperation as the girls all laughed. "He's just a cute cow fitter with a great butt! There's fifty of them in there ready to buy you a drink, Bella!"

"So what are you going to do?"

"I'm gonna keep my options open, that's what!" Savannah said, adjusting the shirt around her slim waist.

———— • ◆ • ————

Savannah was not about to go right back to Tripp's lap, that was for certain. Macy, always the ringleader, pulled her partners in crime towards a couple other guys she knew. Savannah saw Macy's husband, Stetson Rawlings, huddled at a corner table in big-business mode with one of the largest outside investors in the cattle business. Macy was on her own to entertain herself for the night but that was typical.

Sauntering playfully up to the backside of a young guy from Nebraska that Savannah knew only casually, she pushed against him gently as if there was too little room up near the bar. She leaned down, supporting herself with her elbows knowing that the knit top was stretching nicely across her bust. "I take a Crown and 7," she said to a cheeky bar maid in a stained blouse and faded black bowtie.

"That's on us, and anything her friends want, too," announced Marty Styles as he smiled to Macy and Bella.

Bella ordered a Tanqueray and tonic and Macy added a Crown and 7. " She may be naïve, but the girl damn sure knows how to flirt," Bella leaned in to Macy.

"And how to score free booze," Macy added while they burst into giggles. "What's so funny, Ladies?" Chet Adams asked. He, Marty, and a young guy, Mickey, were on the crew for Neilson Ranches. Savannah didn't know the guys well, but she liked the clean-cut good looks and bright intellect in Chet's eyes.

"We're just enjoying the company of our dear friend Savannah Morgan tonight!"

"Yeah and all the free drinks she's scoring since everybody knows about her break-up!" Bella laughed and offered Marty a dazzling smile.

Chet worked his way closer to Savannah and extended his hand as if to shake.

"What's this for?"

"Well, it's for congratulations, Savannah. Let me be one of many to welcome you to the ranks of singledom once again! My divorce was final in September and damn has it been fun!" Chet said as he and Marty toasted beers with a clink of the amber-colored glass bottles.

In a vain attempt to get back into the conversation with the fine looking women, Mickey piped up: "Yeah, you know why divorce is so expensive, don't ya? Its because its worth it!"

Chet reached over and patronizingly patted the younger guy's head. "What do you know? Dude-you're 18-hell you shouldn't even be in here! Me and Marty shouldn't even be buying you beers, so go hit on a high school chick at the kiddy-pool, will ya?"

Everyone laughed. Mickey punched Chet in the shoulder.

Savannah studied Chet for a moment while he badgered the crew's rookie some more. He was tall enough, but not more than an inch taller than her, if that. He was lean and wiry the way truly hard working guys on western ranches were and she could see the taut muscles pulling tensely against his tucked-in plaid shirt. His faded Wrangler's weren't starched and he hadn't bothered to change shoes as evidenced by the small mound of crusty mud that created a little track on the Exec's faded carpet. Looking up at his face, he was handsome with a day's light stubble on his chin and sideburns and a chiseled, almost crooked nose. His eyes were light and wide set, probably blue-grey and his hair was cut neat and short, though he'd obviously worn a hat all day in the barn.

"Have I got something on my face-we ate Mexican-it could be any-thing!" Chet raised a self-conscious hand to his lip and wiped across it.

"No, no, I was noticing how cute you are, that's all," Savannah said and smiled sweetly as she toyed with the yellow drink stirrer in her cock-tail. "Thanks for the drink, Handsome."

"You know, that's B.S.! The chicks always go for Chet and I'm the cute one, you know-come on look at these biceps!" Marty added in mock offense as Bella made a play for touching his arms and being interested.

"You girls want to find a seat somewhere or head over to the Exec West?" Chet asked. He'd seen the move Tripp Crothers had made on Savannah and saw her shocked face, too. He had to work fast-Savannah Morgan was a nice girl - too nice to mess around with a cowboy player like Tripp. "It's getting to be all old people over here these days, anyway."

But, Chet was too late to get the girls away from the competition.

"Hey, I've kept that seat warm for a while now, Savannah," Tripp remarked as he approached and put a possessive arm around her waist. "Chet-thanks for keeping Savannah company for me - I had some stuff to take care of anyway. How's your stock look?" Tripp asked with mock polite interest.

Sometimes Chet wished the damn show cattle deal wasn't so small-everybody pretty much knew everybody else's business. He knew Tripp Crothers because his boss had hired him once and Chet had caught him messing around with owner's 17-year-old daughter. Chet had had a bad opinion of the guy long before he heard that Savannah was a free woman.

Savannah couldn't help but enjoy herself-the smooth drawl of Tripp's voice was like a venerable purr in her ears, the tug of his firm hand nestling her against hip a sexual tension she enjoyed, even the cockiness in Tripp's eyes was hot! She wouldn't be able to stand dating him, but this was just *fun*.

"Savannah-are you getting drunk?" Bella asked, laughing and knowing the answer-Savannah had totally left the conversation.

"I guess I am! Whew, its late, I need to get to the room and hit the bed-its just me and Eddie tomorrow!"

"You want me to walk you up?" Macy asked.

"No, no, I can walk to the third floor-you go locate your spouse and see if he's made you any richer-I'll see you tomorrow, Babes," she said giving both girlfriends light hugs. "Guys, it was fun-thanks for the drinks-we'll hit it again tomorrow, okay?" she said, for some reason directing her eyes to Chet instead of Tripp.

"I'll walk you up," Tripp stated rather than offered. Savannah knew he assumed that this was their exit together. She suddenly decided to go alone.

"No, Tripp - stay, there's still another hour 'til closing time and it's the first night in. Goodnight everybody," Savannah said as Macy crossed the bar looking for Stetson and Bella took a seat next to Marty.

The fresh air of the drafty foyer felt good compared to the nostril-clogging cigarette smoke in the bar. Savannah strode briskly through the winding corridors of the Exec's ancient hallways. She reached a slim hand to grasp the railway of the ramp leading from the banquet facilities to the guestrooms and steadied herself for a moment. She almost laughed at her ridiculous behavior at the bar. She hiccupped and then resumed her wobbly trek. She reached her room and fumbled in the narrow pocket of her slim-fitting jeans for the key. Growing annoyed with her mildly drunken clumsiness, Savannah was unable to properly align the old brass key in the door. She was so engaged in her fight with the wretched device that she didn't notice anyone advance in the empty hallway.

Tripp grasped Savannah roughly around the waist as he pushed aside her hair and savored a taste of her slim neck. Savannah reeled in shock as thousands of unexpected waves of pleasure overtook her flipping and already frothy stomach. Firm arms held her close as Tripp murmured something and turned her to kiss him.

"Tripp!" Savannah gasped and fell against him in the relief of realizing she knew her attacker. Her body sagged tantalizingly against the oak-like strength of his limbs. Tripp didn't pause his exploration of her neck.

"What are you doing here?"

This time Tripp looked up and his steely gaze met hers with an intensity Savannah had never before seen on a man's face. "I liked your exit, but it was difficult to find your room, at least until you couldn't get your key in the door so I caught up!"

"Wait-you followed me here? I didn't mean for that Tripp, I'm sorry if you got the wrong idea," Savannah said, trying to pull back slightly. Her mind was reeling and her body was not listening to good common sense.

Tripp leaned back and ran one thick, calloused hand through his wavy, collar-length hair. He cocked a full brow at her, it arched wickedly above his luminous tawny brown eyes. His other palm firmly, yet seductively, stroked her shoulder and then her collarbone. Savannah felt her insides caving as if she were riding a rollercoaster that was headed straight down. Tripp's leer split his lips, revealing bleached-white teeth and his full, soft mouth. "So, you're saying that you'd like me to leave?"

Savannah hesitated just a moment and Tripp took advantage of her indecision by kissing her.

"Tripp, I, uh, I'm sorry if you got the wrong idea. I've got to get to bed," she said, pushing him back. Miraculously, the key worked. "Maybe tomorrow night?"

"Really?" was all she heard Tripp say as she pulled the door quickly shut. It was a few moments before she heard Tripp sigh heavily and step away from the door.

~ SIX ~

Green Shavings

The ugly red digital numbers swam in the blackness – 6:15. Savannah cringed. She sat up quickly and immediately regretted the rash action.

Uh, I've got a hangover.

She was grateful for the hot water and the fact that three weeks of solid practice had forced her body to wake up without an alarm clock. She gelled her hair with the new blonde-enhancing product everyone was using and wound the long tresses into a tight, wet knot at the nape of her neck. She smoothed her bangs to the side to create some definition around her face. The chignon was mostly a handy summer hairdo for hot, humid days when long hair was like wearing a wreath of wool, but it had to suffice today. With all the fans in the barn, the chignon would dry by noon and she'd pull it down and fluff it into a cute wavy look for the rest of the day.

If only the bags under my eyes were as easy to fix.

By 6:35 Savannah was warming up the truck and waiting for Eddie. His lateness irked her. She was about to call his room when amid the Louisville drizzle and fog, his hand appeared on the door.

"Nice of you to have it warmed up for me," Eddie groused as he slumped into the passenger seat. His shoes were untied and his shirt untucked, but he'd showered at least. "Hey, are we going to stop at McDonald's or something?" he pulled the collar of his down vest around his ears, shivering.

"Not a chance, Eddie, we're both late. You can grab a pop out of the cooler."

Savannah was more than a little nervous about running into Tripp in the barn. What was she going to say to the man she'd snubbed at her door? As she led Tiara out of the misty drizzle and toward the steamy humidity of the barn, she hoped that she'd have at least until after lunch before she saw him.

"Hey check it out," Eddie remarked as they passed the line of people huddled in front of the breakfast food truck. "That nasty Wanda chick must be out of jail again!" Eddie said with a laugh. The scent of bacon made Savannah's stomach turn and the sight of Wanda, cow showing's resident lot lizard, dumping out a grease trap made vomit catch in her throat.

At least my life hasn't gotten that bad, she thought.

Comparing morning and evening at a stock show was at an interesting study in contrasts. It was impossible to call the barn quiet-raging fans, hungry bawling cattle, and the whine of blowers started off every morning. Somewhere near Morgan Cattle Company's stalls a high school boy was blasting CREED on his boom box as fuel-powered generators popped and pulled power to supplement what had to be an astronomical amount of electricity required to power two weeks of livestock exhibition. Still, in the hours between 5 and 11 am as exhibitors readied their livestock for a new day, the barn's ambiance was one of relative calm. Everyone was busy so people mostly passed by with a wave or stopped by for just a moment, rather than idle away thirty minutes or more as they would in the afternoon and evening. In the morning, the barns were only a place for those who worked. The absentee owners, investors, moms with little kids, grand parents, general boozers, and showbox kids (as Savannah called those youngsters that showed up just in time to lead one into the ring), were not present when the real work of the day was done.

As the sun rose and bloomed into morning outside, indoors the barns came awake with cattle fitters making all the necessary adjustments to make the stock better than the day before. They adjusted rations, adding or subtracting feed and supplements depending on the attitudes of stock, added products to make them eat, take away bloating, aid in digestion, or help one that had gotten sick. All cattle were washed, dried, then brushed and groomed with oils and sprays to a glossy sheen. Hard workers might labor over an hour on just one head to achieve the desired look. Better haired cattle were even valued at a premium and easier to get looking right since straight hair was much preferred over wavy.

If you could work a Hereford's curly hair, you could work on a cross-bred any day.

Owners evaluated their stock against their neighbors and their competition, discussing which way to clip or shear even the shortest hairs in the hope that an animal might look just enough better to sell for more in the sale or place higher in the show. Instructions like: 'take this neckline down a bit', or 'neaten up the underline and flank', or 'carve more round to her stifle' were commonly heard. Decisions were made in the morning about matters such as who would lead in the ring, which heifers might get scratched from the list and not make the show, and how to get the cattle looking their best. Morning, too, was the time to evaluate anything that might lead to a big sale or a purple banner. All across the barn the fine details were being discussed as many, like Savannah, put their own lack of sleep aside in the quest to make the stock as comfortable and as attractive as possible. Guys often said they'd rather be the cow at the show than the cow fitter. Most show cattle animals were more Primadonna than the prissiest of pageant queens. In the barn, show cattle came first.

Most stalls boasted displays of past winners, donor cows, and high quality progeny in picture books or tabletop displays. Everyone had by now hung their pedigree signs and the placards labeled with each cow's pedigree information danced in the drafty barn where they were hung above the stalls.

Savannah had done a good job of staying at her stalls all morning and avoiding any gossip from the night before until about 11:30 when Eddie came walking back from the bathroom. He'd warmed up working in the humid barn and had removed his button down shirt to reveal one of those tacky 'co-ed naked cattle fitting' t-shirts it like everybody was wearing. The heifers were resting comfortably and Savannah was straightening up her area, running a broom and trying to act low key. She figured Macy would be over any minute to discuss whatever rumor Tripp might have cultivated to save face, but it was Eddie who got to the subject first.

"Whew, Savannah! Now that's some funny stuff you pulled on Tripp Crothers!" Eddie literally bent over and slapped his knee as he reached to the cooler for a beer. Savannah looked at her watch; never to early, she supposed. She'd still have to get him to change his shirt.

"What are you talking about?" Savannah asked, remaining composed-she figured an elaborate lie was about to be heard.

"Tripp Crothers just informed me that I had a hot boss, but she sure wasn't putting out! He said you took him upstairs but wouldn't let him in your room! I bet that doesn't happen to the cocky jerk much! Serves him right."

Though it wasn't exactly an attractive or genteel rendition of what transpired, it was mostly accurate and for that Savannah was grateful.

"I didn't mean to take it far at all, in fact, I went to bed by myself and he followed me." Savannah said as she absently unwound the coiled hair band a move that spilled damp, wavy blonde hair about her shoulders. She stood silently for a moment noticing the way Eddie watched her as she dug her fingers through the strands in an effort to style them.

"So, Crothers wasn't lying?"

Savannah chortled and reached into the cooler herself.

A little hair of the dog will go a long way to making me feel better.

"Nope, nothing happened."

Eddie felt relieved. "Well, I'm glad to hear there's nothing to report!"

"Report to who, Eddie?"

"Oh, just an expression-you know- like 'no news is good news' or something. At least no one will be gossiping about you too much now because Tripp won't want this getting around about him!"

Just then Savannah turned at the sound of a feminine voice calling her name. Macy was striding briskly toward them, water bottle in one hand, designer purse swinging from the other. Eddie groaned and turned away to busy himself with his clippers in a vain attempt to pretend they needed oiled.

"Savannah! O MY GOD! Girl-you are soo baaad!" Macy cooed. Savannah had always enjoyed Macy as a friend, but she felt an odd twinge of jealously that the woman obviously didn't have to work between coming from old land money in Texas and marrying old oil money from Oklahoma. She dripped sterling silver and turquoise accessories and looked stunning in a tight leather jacket and starched crisp white blouse, her mahogany-colored hair styled in wild wisps around her heart shaped face and her make up, though loud and heavily applied, was perfectly set evidencing that fact that she, unlike Savannah, had neither risen at 6:15 am to walk heifers into the barn in the rain nor had she rinsed, brushed, and blown on the calves in the humid barn since 7:00. While Savannah's cheeks bore a slight flush from the effort and the humidity, Macy had the palette-perfect face of a woman that just stepped away from the M.A.C. counter.

"OH MY GOD!" she announced again. "Get me a beer and tell me how you managed to up-stage Tripp Crothers! Bella is going to D-I-E, die! She'd also D-I-E to get in Tripp's pants and he's never noticed her, of course, and then you take him upstairs and kick him out before he gets his pants off! That is too funny!" Macy flung herself in a Morgan Cattle Company embroidered director's chair. Reaching into her purse, she produced a cowhide-covered koozie that was studded with sterling and coral beads. "Isn't this thing adorable? I bought it last December in Reno - I'll get you a couple - now talk, Girl!"

At the prospect of their girl talk, Eddie mumbled something about needing to see a man about a horse. He didn't need to hear about whatever *did* happen.

Savannah had just started to recount the night's final events when she saw Bella heading for them with a look of bewildered amusement lighting up her pretty freckled face. "I'll grab another beer," Macy said.

The afternoon passed quickly with Savannah spending about half of it laughing with her girlfriends. Tripp wandered by once and shook his head as if to imply that he was devastated by her rejection, a move that sent the girls bursting into giggles.

By 3:30 potential buyers for the next day's sale were coming around to peruse stock. She called Eddie signaling for him to come back to the stalls and get Tiara up. Maybe they could even sell a flush on her private treaty if the right person happened by. Harlan hadn't wanted to use embryo transfer, it was just one of the outdated ways about which he was stubborn, but Savannah was ready to move into using more advanced technology. Some people even split flushes, so maybe doing that with a buyer would be a way for her to learn something new and get some embryos. If she was going to act grown up at a cattle show, it was time she stared having these kinds of conversations with prospective buyers.

Shoppers at a livestock show come in every stripe, with all kinds of different goals in mind, and certainly with every size of checkbook. Ranging from 4-H families without much experience and aspirations only to win their home county fair, to those that wanted a clubby heifer for 'jackpot' points shows, to traders hoping to buy calves cheap, mark them up, and re-sell them, finally to breeders seeking to add new genetics to their own herds, there was a buyer for most any animal.

Every one of them might see the same heifer differently.

People's ability to cut a good deal varied widely, too. There were the easy-to-read types that showed their hands way too early and were marks for the more unscrupulous cattle resellers. By sharp contrast, some experienced traders were smart about buying and selling – they knew what a heifer was worth and just how quickly they could get that amount made back. They could be good clients-if you could get them to pay. Buyers that would 'speak for' a heifer with the intention of reselling it first before paying the original owner made for an on-going problem in the cattle business. Sometimes the same animal would change hands three or four times with a trader trying to make money on each transaction.

Savannah didn't yet have her father's knack for dealing with people, though she did possess her mother's intuition, a trait that would be helpful discerning people's whims and buying signals. She needed to hone her negotiation skills, that was certain.

By tie-out time, Savannah was famished and ready for dinner. She grabbed Tiara's halter and headed to the center aisle that led to the exit. Up ahead she saw Neilson Ranches Nebraska crew pulling out with their Shorthorn cattle.

"Eddie, I'm going to catch up with them, I'll meet you back here – would you start on cleaning the stalls?" she asked, pushing Tiara to trot as she strode hard to overtake Neilson's crew.

Chet and Mickey were at the rear with Marty leading a stout 2-year-old bull at the head of their group. Savannah didn't know why, but she felt like she ought to talk to Chet. "Hey, Nebraska!" she called. Chet turned around and grinned-he'd heard about Tripp Crothers' crash and burn and had wanted to talk with Savannah all day. Since the stalking method hadn't worked with Tripp he didn't want to get too aggressive. He wanted to date Savannah; he wasn't a user like Tripp.

"I just wanted to catch up and see where you were going for dinner," Savannah said, falling in beside him.

"We're going for Mexican at 'El Cap Your Ass' - you and Eddie wanna come?" Chet asked using the vernacular name for the popular Mexican place that featured good but exceeding spicy Mexican food.

"Yeah, probably, I'll ask him." Savannah and Chet chatted easily as they made the half-mile walk to the tie-outs.

Parting ways at her trailer, Savannah left the Neilson Ranch guys, pulled Tiara's halter off, and turned her into the night pen as she spread some fresh hay. She double checked the padlock on the gate and started back toward the barn to help Eddie clean stalls. As she maneuvered through the vast lot jammed with trucks, trailers, semis, and cattle, darkness settled over the scene and a soft haze softened the landscape that was lit only with the occasional blue-white glow of a security light. Walking through yet another cluster of makeshift pens, she heard a voice call out from behind a sleek, new Farrell's brand trailer.

"Savannah! Hey-come 'ere!"

"Who is it?" Savannah asked, amused and unafraid.

"Its me, Tripp! I've got to hide my face since you shunned me!"

Savannah laughed and stepped into the shadow of the trailer. Tripp was inside leaning against a stall gate. He had obviously been taking a leak.

"What are you doing?" She stepped up into the trailer and moved toward Tripp.

He pulled her into his arms. Without a word from either of them he kissed her and she kissed back. "Hey, last night was fun, but you know, it didn't end how I had hoped," he said huskily and kissed her again.

"Well, you don't always get every girl you want, Tripp Crothers," Savannah said and this time she initiated a soft, slow kiss.

"Tonight we're going to be a little late, the limo is picking us up at 8:00 for Trixie's , but maybe later this week we could finish what we started last night?"

Savannah cringed at the thought that she was kissing a man who in less than an hour would have his hands all over some stripper. "We'll see what happens, Tripp, no promises, though," she said and with a flip peck on his cheek she waved goodbye and trotted off toward the barn. She had dinner plans with Bachelor Number Two-the easy and safe Chet.

———————————•◆•———————————

Eddie was more than happy to eat dinner with the low-key guys form Neilson Ranches and for once he seemed at ease as Savannah watched him guzzle margaritas and laugh with Mickey and Marty over some crude story Savannah didn't want to hear anyway. She was seated next to Chet at the other end of the table. How they had gotten separated from the raucous "fun" part of the group, Savannah wasn't sure, but she knew Chet had planned to keep her to himself. Not that she minded the pleasant, sensible conversation with Chet or the way he looked at her with blind devotion; it was just a little much though. She knew without asking that Chet could get serious. They enjoyed their own pitcher of margaritas causing Savannah to get really sleepy. By 10:30, the crew was planning to go to the seedy Double Deuce bar next, but Savannah knew she needed to get to bed. Tomorrow was show day. She had to be "on", not looking like death warmed over. She said as much to Chet, who smiled warmly and offered to drive her back to the Exec.

"Eddie, I'm turning in. If you're going to the Double Deuce, you might as well not go to bed 'cause I'm waking you up at 4:30 and we're going to be walking Tiara into the barn at 5:00," Savannah said as she strode over and put a firm hand on Eddie's shoulder. She knew he was having fun and wasn't interested in her demands.

"How you gettin' back to the hotel?" he asked without looking up.

"I'm giving her a ride," Chet assured and much to Savannah's dismay he placed a friendly, but possessive arm around her shoulders.

"Oh, well, I guess that's fine with me," Eddie grumbled and looked away.

Savannah rolled her eyes and just hoped he'd be sober enough to help her rinse in the morning.

Against her better judgment, Savannah didn't decline when Chet offered to walk her upstairs. She was attracted to him, but she could see the feelings written all over his face and didn't want to drag him into something that she didn't want to finish. Still, he was a grown man and surely he could understand that she wasn't looking for anything serious. At least she hoped he understood that, but all through dinner Chet had been talking about how he liked marriage and wanted the right woman to come into his life. She had clarified for him that while she was completely done with Troy and filed for divorce, he was making it difficult and she didn't know how long it was going to take. Chet was unphased about the legal details, Savannah could tell. Either way, no matter how long it took to unload Troy, Savannah couldn't imagine how awful it would be to move to an isolated ranch back where Chet was from.

She definitely wasn't going to end up his wife.

Still, she was enjoying his company and liked the sweet, adoring way he looked at her. Chet was a wonderful bandage for her bruised ego and lonely soul.

"Well, here we are, thanks for walking me up, Chet," Savannah said looking him in the eye and wondering if he'd try something like Tripp had the night before. He didn't, Chet was too sincere for that.

"Its no problem, Savannah. I had a great time at dinner with you. I have to say something-you're absolutely gorgeous-but you don't even know it, do you?" he edged closer, but not so close that Savannah felt her personal space compromised.

Savannah blushed slightly at the intense sincerity of his compliment. To tell him that she had never thought herself even remotely close to gorgeous seemed an insult to his heartfelt statement. So she said simply: "You're kind, Chet, that's sweet."

"I'm not sweet, Savannah. I'm just a simple cow fitter from middle-of-nowhere-Nebraska, but I do tell the truth, and the truth is you're beautiful," Chet stated again, not allowing her gaze to drop off. He reached his hands out gently and took hers in his as he moved two steps closer. His eyes were a bluish hazel color with flecks of green. His nose, Savannah noticed at this close range, was slightly crooked, but attractive; he'd probably broken it. His smile was broad and genuine.

Savannah surprised them both when she put her head on his shoulder and her arms around his back. Chet was comfortable and strong and it felt so good to be near him. He sighed softly and pulled his arms tighter around her in a hug and kissed the top of her head. Savannah loved the feeling of being held, something she realized no man had done since the last hug she received from her Dad. The thought made her shiver and feel overwhelmingly sad. Suddenly, Savannah felt terribly alone. Swallowing hard, to the point that it hurt, she pushed the tears and loneliness down firmly with the lump in her throat. Pushing back she mouthed 'good night" as she stepped inside the privacy of her hotel room to cry.

———————— •◆• ————————

Tiara must have sensed that it was show morning.

Like girl, like show-cow, Savannah mused.

The big heifer was antsy and fought at the halter as she seemed to race in from tie-outs. Savannah knew her own nerves were making the heifer act up.

It was her day to win with Tiara.

After the disappointment of being left standing at Kansas City, Savannah was banner hungry.

She wanted to win Louisville - wanted to win Denver, too, - it would be the last show before Tiara was turned out to calve. No, what she really wanted, Savannah thought, was to have won the Triple Crown, but with being passed over at the Royal, she had just two chances left. A win at Louisville would be impressive for the sake of winning a major in the Midwest. A win at Denver was like taking home a Super Bowl title. But, honestly, the venue didn't matter; everybody wanted to win them all.

Savannah felt the aura in the barn shift from previous mornings, the taut feeling of out-to-get-you competiveness was now pervasive. It wasn't unfamiliar; the anomaly of best friends one day and fierce competitors the next was typical. Cattle people were just different on show days. The big leagues like Louisville could be cut throat.

By 8 am, the misty haze from livestock grooming products had turned to an impenetrable fog. Fitters would now be in high demand until as late as 9 or 10 that night for some of the larger breeds shows. Paint in red, white, and black would hang in the humid, stale air while it was applied where nature had not been so perfect with the desired color of an animal's hide, where a flaw needed amending, or where a stain from grass, or manure needed a touch up. At day's end, even those not crawling around with a set of shears to block out of calf's leg hair would be black-nosed from the sheer amount of products circulating in the air. Now was time to employ the tricks of the trade and secrets of the best fitters. A good fitter could expect a day wage of over $200, but commonly the quick-hire grunts received $50 to $100 or took some help on their own stock in trade. All that mattered today, show day, was the cattle themselves and, of course, politics.

Politics, Savannah thought, were both a nemesis and a fact of showing cattle. The practice was the industry's cog in the wheel. Harlan hadn't played them much and had always lived by the belief that somehow the best cattle would sort themselves to the top of the class. Savannah felt the view was antiquated. Spending plenty of money at certain judge's production sale could go a long way to ensuring a good look in the show ring. Savannah thought it was too bad, shoddy, perhaps, but she wasn't naïve enough to believe that she'd win on high quality stock alone. Looking around, she vowed to do a better job of 'getting connected' to the right people, as Macy put it. Stetson was an ace at networking and he judged a lot of shows, too, so as a result the bulls he sold went high and Rawlings Ranch usually went home with banners. Still, Savannah *knew* her heifer was one of the best in the barn, maybe even in the breed. Tiara had the look that it should take to win; she was moderate framed and deep sided. Sound as a cat, she stood on plenty of bone, but not so much that it made her look rugged. She was good enough fronted for a Hereford and great haired.

She was in the hunt today. Making the backdrop was the only objective.

Savannah had hired another guy to help Eddie fit and she watched them as they pulled Tiara out of the stall and moved her to an aluminum grooming chute where she'd stand as her legs, body hair, and top were clipped, combed, and sprayed with product to hold the perfect hairs in place. Meanwhile, Savannah changed into a slim-fitting button down top, put on her best pieces of sterling jewelry, and added a Kippy's-brand sparkle belt. She donned her best boots, $400 Ostrich Lucchese's that she saved for show days, and pulled the sides of her hair up with a silver clip. Back at the stall, she placed her exhibitor number into custom-made leather show harness that fit over her shoulders like a vest. She checked for her lucky show stick-that was a must.

Noticing the heifer was nearly ready, she quickly polished a brown leather show halter then traded it for the plain rope halter Tiara wore when not in the ring. She rubbed the heifer behind the ears. "It's our day, it's our day," she whispered.

"Hereford exhibitors, be bringing those junior yearling heifers to the make-ready area!" bellowed an announcer from the show ring. Savannah took a deep breath. She loved to show, loved everything about it, but something about the moments before she entered the ring always made her nervous deep down inside. It was ridiculous, but she was always overcome with an urge to pee right before she led a calf to the ring. As if on cue with the announcer, she felt butterflies take flight in the pit of her stomach. She knew some girls that got so nervous before a show that they actually tried to get a little drunk to calm down. She considered it-Eddie had a bottle of Crown Royal in the showbox-but she didn't want to be nauseous *and* nervous so she ran to the bathroom for a second time instead.

Pulling Tiara from the stalls, Eddie checked her once more and then they navigated out into the main aisle. It was a job getting through with all the other chutes, extension cords, and cattle going back and forth, but Tiara was unalarmed by sidestepping fitters sprawled underneath other cattle. The aisles were always like this on show day, but there were a couple of rules: clean up your own manure and leave your scotch combs tines down.

Emerging from the dimly lit walkway that gave on to the show ring, the brilliance of the high-powered fluorescent lights beamed in every direction. Savannah walked slowly down the ramp taking her first steps on Louisville's famous green shavings, the verdant carpet of green bedding lay before them covered by a sea of red and white cattle. Potted plants and Americana banners perfectly lined the white fence of the show ring. Jaunty organ music, played by the same lady for as long as Savannah could remember, lent a festive air to the big arena while the announcer's radio-smooth voice presented the winners from the previous class. Savannah felt the nervousness rise in her throat once again as she eyed the competition. She knew she'd have to show against twelve or so heifers since the January division was always popular. The heifer that won Kansas City was there and she looked good. It would be tough to get around her, but it was doable. The rest of the field looked average.

As she waited for the class, Eddie recombed Tiara and Savannah rubbed her brisket absently with a show stick, the steady, repetitive motion calming her as much as her heifer. The reserve in Kansas City had not made it to the show; she'd been a bit of a surprise pick in the Grand line up, anyway, Savannah thought.

I should have won at least Reserve, she reflected as she adjusted her belt and tucked her blouse in tighter.

The game was on!

———————— •◆• ————————

Louisville, KY, 1999

Show Day

The few laps around the ring that should have gone perfectly were far from it as Tiara balked at the decorations along the fence and wouldn't place her front feet correctly when parked for the judge's first look. By the time they were ready to stop again, another heifer ran up on them too close and pushed Savannah and Tiara out of the line up. Just when the judge could have gotten another nice profile, Savannah was partially obstructed and forced to circle and reset. Before Savannah could get her placed again, he pulled the Kansas City champion into first.

There goes Grand, already!

Savannah started to panic. She reached her lead arm out long and checked Tiara as she pushed the heifer's head forward a bit more. The judge walked past her, but she couldn't catch his eye. He was a big, florid-faced Canadian that Savannah didn't know. It was as if he'd never even looked at her! She wished for the tenth time that day that Harlan had done more politicking. It was too late for that now - all she had was this moment.

She hated to do it, but she had to get his attention, so she tugged on Tiara's halter, pulled her way out into the ring and started to circle her back

71

into a new pose. This time, the judge paused and evaluated her, as if seeing her for the first time.

Finally!

She finished pulling her back in and resetting her, never once taking her eyes off the judge. She knew she had shadowed the heifer behind her more than was polite, but that just couldn't be helped.

Come on, come on!

Suddenly, to her horror, she saw him pull a soggy, plain-necked female into second while immediately waving her to third.

Savannah was crestfallen, she hadn't given that heifer a single thought. She was probably nice enough to wander the pastures of some no-named commercial herd, but this was a national show!

I've got the show heifer in the ring, for God's sake!

Trying her best not to act furious and stunned, she followed to her placing as the judge continued his selections.

Louisville was lost.

~ SEVEN ~

Cattle Showing – By Day and By Night

It was almost 11:00 when she saw Chet stroll into the Exec's bar and he made a beeline for her table.

"Hey. How bad?" he asked easing into the seat Macy vacated to let him have.

"Third." Chet put his arm around her shoulders.

Third was the cruelest placing. It wasn't last and it meant the judge probably liked your female well enough, but not well enough to get you in the hunt. It was the placing the judge stuffed you in when he didn't want to see you again that day.

Really, all it meant was a chance at nothing but a disappointing ride home.

Savannah had been practically inconsolable all afternoon. She wanted to hide in the room and pout, but Macy's urging for just one round coaxed her into a least coming downstairs for a while.

"Hey, you want to get out of here?" Chet asked, putting his hand over hers.

"Sure. You know what? I've got a really uncomfortable old couch in my room and a bottle of wine. Two plastic cups and we've got it made," she said, knowing Chet would be overjoyed.

Upstairs Savannah cleared the cramped space by throwing clothes and coats over the old radiator while Chet adjusted himself on the cramped couch and tried to look relaxed.

"I don't know why they even put couches in these tiny rooms," Savannah commented as she opened the bottle of California Cabernet.

"I guess they just made them for people like you and me and times like these." They talked for one glass about the day's activities and how Neilson's had to show the next morning with their Shorthorns. Chet wasn't even going to bed since they had to be at the barn by 2:30. Neilson's ran a big string of 20 head so someone would literally be on and off the wash rack all day between rinsing before and after the show.

After the second glass, it was Chet who made the first move. His kiss was warm and deep from the start and Savannah yielded to it immediately, thoroughly enjoying the combination of security and sensuality that she felt as she pressed against Chet's chest. He caressed her face, her eyes, and touched her mouth as he arched her slightly over the back of the stiff little couch. She let out of soft moan and said his name and Chet sighed and told her again how beautiful she was and how good her body felt in his arms. She could kiss Chet all night, but by the way he moved on top of her, she knew she had to cut it off before she was writing checks she never intended to cash. Pulling back, she again leaned into his strong shoulders. If he was disappointed, he didn't show it while he stroked her hair.

Sometime after 2:00 Chet covered her with the bedspread and left for the barn.

He knew only one thing; he was in love.

———————————— • ◆ • ————————————

The show's policy, though nobody liked it, dictated that exhibitors couldn't leave until all breed shows were over, so Savannah and Eddied had two full days to hang out without obligations. The cattle were technically supposed to be brought into the barn daily, even after they'd shown, but nobody hurried much about it. Savannah spent her day doing a little shopping at the expo center and then hanging out with Macy as they watched Bella and the Neilson Ranches show Shorthorns. By evening, Neilson's crew had invited them to dinner again. Eddie was beginning to notice Savannah and Chet, especially when they declined going with the rest of the crew to the Double Deuce to celebrate Neilson's win in the bull show. Savannah knew people were talking but thankfully nobody on the crew made crude remarks when they skipped out early. Savannah couldn't help but feel a little guilty as she kissed Chet and led him to her room; she knew her intentions with him were entirely selfish and she hoped that he didn't get hurt. He was just so sweet and handsome and fun to be around.

"I'm leaving tomorrow morning with the crew, you know," he began propping himself up on one arm and scratching at his neatly cropped hair. Their crew was large enough that half of them took tack home early while the other half stayed with the stock.

"Yeah, I know," was all Savannah managed.

"Well, what's going to happen with us?"

"Chet, I'm still married. Believe me, I'm trying to get divorced from Troy, but for now, it's just not right," Savannah hoped in vain that it could be the end of the conversation.

"You haven't been behaving very married, Savannah, of course I'm the only one you're allowed to behave this way with, though," Chet said as he leaned down and kissed the tip of her nose. Savannah felt herself stiffen.

What the hell did he mean 'what she was allowed to do?'

Hadn't she just explained that this couldn't go anywhere-that she didn't want or need another man to claim he had a possession of her?

Chet felt her pull back. "What wrong, Baby? Did I say something wrong?"

Savannah thought the reference to a grown woman as 'baby' was ridiculous and vile. She stiffened again; she didn't want to hurt Chet.

Maybe I should just go on and get it over with.

Chet didn't allow that logical thing to happen though as he leaned back down and drew her into his arms again, his eyes beseeching with an imploring look.

Oh, no, Chet, she thought. *Please don't say what I think you're going to say...*

"Savannah, I know this is soon, and I know there are complications, but I, well, I , I think I'm in love with you."

———————— ◆ ————————

The next day when Chet called for the third time, Savannah ignored her phone again.

Tripp was absolutely cracking everyone up over a story about his crew barely eluding the police and somebody getting sick in the truck's cup holders. Savannah didn't know what to say to Chet and it felt somewhere between awful and irritating. It had been a mistake to get involved with someone so sweet and vulnerable. She knew he was serious and she wasn't, but the last thing she needed was to be tied down when she wasn't even out from underneath her mess with Troy. Still, she thought she needed to at least say something to him, so she excused herself from the small group that had crowded coolers around for seats and stepped out to answer her cell.

"What's going on? I've been trying you all day, but you haven't answered!" Chet sounded frantic, much to Savannah's immediate annoyance.

"I don't know, Chet. Early this morning I couldn't hear my phone over the noise in the barn, and I just saw that you called. How's the drive going?" Savannah asked, trying to keep the conversation light.

"Why don't you tell me what's going on, Savannah, I know you've been sitting at Tripp Crothers' stall all afternoon and having a good time with him, too, I hear-"

Savannah ceased listening and glanced around. The hair on the back of her neck rose as if she were being tracked in a forest. She felt uncomfortable where moments ago she'd been laughing and carrying on playfully. Had Chet convinced someone to spy on her? She couldn't believe the man's nerve.

I can talk to whomever I want to!

"Savannah, Savannah-" Chet was saying when she turned her attention back to his call. Savannah's response was quick and brutal. "Chet, I'm sorry if you got the wrong idea about us, but you had no right to have me followed. I don't have anything else to say." She folded her phone in half then switched it off. She had a tinge of guilt about being so cold with Chet, but he started it and she was ending it.

Savannah flounced back into the barn tossing long blonde hair over her shoulders and ruffling bangs to create fetching wisps about her face. She unzipped her lime green puff vest and unfastened one more button on her snug fitting blouse. She smoothed her jeans and reached into her pocket for lip-gloss.

Chet Adams has no rights over me! Savannah thought indignantly. *No man does!*

Macy recognized the look of solid defiance on her friend's face and immediately regretted telling Chet that she'd keep him posted. She shouldn't have done it; she didn't mean to stir trouble, only to help Chet out-he was a nice guy and Savannah deserved a nice guy- but it had been a mistake that was going to back fire for both of her friends.

Eddie, too, watched carefully as Savannah instantly became flirty with Tripp when she returned from her phone call. It had to either be her husband or Chet to tick her off that much and he knew she wouldn't have taken Troy's call. Eddie reached under his hat and ran the flat of his palm across his smooth head. He felt sick. The Nielsen crew had been crudely speculating about Savannah and Chet but Eddie tried to ignore it. The guys shut up fast though if Chet was near; he'd nearly knocked Marty's block off for a silly remark about Savannah looking good in jeans. If Chet was so protective, Eddie knew they were having a thing. Savannah had more man problems-and options-than one girl needed. The sad thing was, Eddie knew he wasn't even on her radar.

Savannah was ready to party. She had a restlessness about her that she knew could only lead a young lady for trouble or at least to a bad reputation. Jessica would be scandalized at the thoughts Savannah was entertaining about Tripp as she primped for the evening. But, it was her last night of fun. Returning home meant winter without her father and dealing with her divorce. In some ways she dreaded it all, but that couldn't be helped. She was alone now in the world and sorry she'd made such a fool of herself curled up in Chet's arms. Before she got down to the business of being in charge of Morgan Cattle Company she was going to enjoy the last night in town.

The annual Steer Party, as it was known, was just the place to accomplish her goal of riding the 'sin wagon' home. The Grand and Reserve Champion market animals would be auctioned off for big money. Buyers and gawkers, auctioneers and cattle enthusiasts, all gathered to see how much money the owners had raised for the animals this year. The steers could fetch in excess of $30,000-a nice sum for something that across the stockyards' scales wouldn't bring 1,000 bucks. The Steer Party was complete with a live band and pricey cocktails giving cowboys and cowgirls all the fuel needed to get into the type of trouble Savannah was planning to find.

Having changed into a brown lace shirt with long bell sleeves and an open collar, she added amber jewelry that she'd purchased that day in the Expo Center. Macy had lent her a pair of Lucky jeans, saying that it was time Savannah gave up on Rocky Mountains like the rest of the show circuit already had. Savannah admitted the lower rise pants were much more comfortable, at least. She'd spent an absurd amount of time on her hair, though when she arrived in Macy's room, she wondered why she bothered-Macy looked like a thousand bucks and her outfit was surely worth much more. Every hair was perfectly gelled into place, every eyelash curled and lacquered to the hilt. Macy's fashionable look and unlimited checkbook could not be rivaled for total cow show couture.

"Hey, I thought Stetson was waiting on us to go over," Savannah began, resisting the time she assumed Macy would waste on additional needless primping.

"Oh, he is, but we need one for the road!" Macy poured a shot of Crown Royal for Savannah and one for herself. The girls tossed them back and shook their heads like college freshman as the liquor burned their throats.

"Whew! That's stout! I made us a cocktail, too," Macy handed Savannah a plastic hotel cup of whiskey mixed with pop and grabbed a Coach-brand wristlet off the desk.

"You ready?"

The girls hustled down the hall, pausing twice to take healthy gulps of a beverage they only had five minutes to finish.

Stetson had acquired free admission to the party from one of his many connections and they quickly met up with Bella and made their way to the bar.

"That one's on me, Ladies!" called a twangy voice from over Savannah's shoulders. Tripp laid a $20 bill down for their cocktails. Leaning into Savannah he said huskily. "They're all on me tonight if that's what it takes to get you on me!"

Savannah cried out in mock offense. He grabbed her arm and forced it lightly behind her back in a playful wrestling pose. "They're a lot more moves like this one if you want to see them. You just didn't give me a chance the other night and then you got all in love with Chet," Tripp said, feigning hurt.

Savannah spun around and looked up at him, her heart skipping. It was such fun to flirt with Tripp because he loved the chase. "I'm not in love with Chet! I'm here to have fun!

"Damn glad to hear it! Now, let me show you how well I do the Texas two-step!" he said, whirling her onto the dance floor the moment the band played their first downbeat.

Savannah and Tripp danced four songs without pause. She wasn't a westerner by birth, but had danced plenty of two-step and swing in country bars during college. She was exhilarated and hadn't had so much fun in years-probably not since college, she realized, having spent the previous four years being married to someone she didn't like and working a job she hated.

I'm sick of being so boring!

She was reeling from the musk of Tripp's cologne and the naughty remarks he made in her ear every time they drew close. She needed to slow down and get some water.

"I haven't two-stepped in forever!" Savannah yelled to Bella over the din of the crowd. "Wow! This is fun!"

Tripp was suddenly behind her with a firm arm on her shoulder. "Whenever you're ready for more dancing-or anything else-you let me know!" he wetly kissed her ear lobe.

Macy, Bella and Savannah sat at their table laughing and talking about whatever came to mind-gossip mostly. As if on cue, Tripp continued to appear and bring her a fresh drink or to entice her into another dance.

She'd become wildly flirtatious and knew she was damn drunk. Whatever guilt or shame over the potential of being a loose a woman was pushed far back into her mind, away from the dim lights of the party, the loud music, and her own justifications.

By 1:00 the band was folding up and the bouncers were blinking the lights. Drunk revelers were cringing at the brightness and hustling out. Eddie had been playing poker at a corner table with a crew out of Iowa when he saw Savannah walking out the door, stumbling drunk, on the arm of Tripp Crothers. Eddie threw his hand down and started to go after her, but he knew it would be a fight with Tripp this time of night. She wasn't worth it to him.

Let her sleep with that son-of-a-bitch, Eddie thought bitterly.

Eddie was disgusted. He had done all he could for her and she saw him only as a friend of convenience and a barn hand at the show. It was all 'Eddie do this' and 'Eddie do that!' 'Eddie clip, lead, brush, feed, scoop crap!' He was burnt.

He gathered what was left of his money and left the game.

Tripp helped Savannah into the passenger side of his Ford King Ranch, literally picking her legs up and placing them on the floorboards. She smiled coyly and leaned into his broad torso while he pulled her into a kiss. She wrapped her arms around his neck more for support than passion.

I am bombed, she thought.

Tripp found a parking spot on a grassy hill in the Exec's overcrowded lot and before Tripp could prevent it, Savannah fell out of the truck and landed in the mud. Tripp lifted her up and helped her into the hotel. In the elevator he was all hands and Savannah didn't care. He groped and pulled away her blouse as he held her backside firmly with the other hand. They clamored down the hallway to her room and when she fumbled with the key, Tripp turned her to him and kissed her again.

"Seems to me we've been here before, Savannah," he rumbled huskily against her neck. "Only this time I'm hoping the outcome will be much better."

"I think we can arrange that, Tripp," Savannah pushed into the room and promptly fell against the wall. Tripp kicked the door shut with a bang. Savannah smiled, though her head hurt from slamming it. Tripp's kisses were intense and getting sloppy and he was lustily saying something about how she was far too much woman for a nice guy like Chet. Savannah considered defending Chet, but it didn't matter, everything was just so fluffy and blurry. She realized that she was sitting or laying down and didn't know why as she felt her boots come off and the coolness of the room breeze past her toes. Tripp was there, kissing her almost savagely, though Savannah was getting sleepy enough not to care. The bed seemed as if it had swallowed her up in it and she was floating down deeper and deeper.

"Hey, don't get tired on me, Babe-we're just getting started," Tripp said in the sexiest version of his natural Texas accent he could muster. He bent over her and shook her lightly.

"Oh, Tripp, you're so hot, aren't you," Savannah began deliriously as she tried to sit up on her elbows. Her whiskey drunk was strong and it had dulled absolutely everything to a whirling, spinning world that swooshed and sloshed in her vision like little scenes in a silent movie. "You're the guy everyone wants. You know Bella would like to have sex with you, Tripp," Savannah went on ridiculously, "But Macy says that you think I'm the hottie of the group-is that true? Tripp-do you think I'm hot?"

Tripp frowned knowing the girl was entirely too drunk to know what the hell was next. He was at a critical point. She'd probably assume they had sex the next day, but she wouldn't remember it. Dark thoughts entered his mind, but he pushed them aside. Still, it infuriated him that twice in one week the best looking catch in the barn had thwarted him. He looked at her longingly, she did look good, but he wasn't some weird-o that screwed asleep girls, and anyway, every guy in the barn would assume he did. He just wouldn't say otherwise.

By the time his boots were back on, Savannah was snoring.

PART II

At the farm

~ EIGHT ~

Intruders

The remaining leaves hung against the drab November sky as if left there in spindly discontent. The sun hadn't shone in what seemed like two weeks and they'd received enough rain to flood the creek bed, prompting Savannah to realize that she needed to move the cows out of the area or they'd sink in the thick mire. She wished it would either warm up and dry out or just go ahead and freeze. Constant damp weather made for a host of cattle problems.

She had taken to riding out to the pasture every evening at dusk. Throwing her legs over the 4-wheeler, she walked to a stump and sat, the dampness of the wet wood slowly seeping through her jeans. Being home from the Louisville show for a few days had continued to strengthen her resolve about the farm. She was determined to see things through and it lifted her spirit. Dusk light always calmed her though it was meager in the colorless late fall doldrums.

She was generally ashamed of herself since Louisville; she had behaved like a tramp. Her mother, for all her shortcomings as a supporter, certainly did not raise her to carry on like a loose woman and she would have never, *ever,* run around like that if her Harlan had been alive. Of course, she always had loads of fun at shows, but she'd never been one of *those* girls. Savannah had been one of those girls at Louisville. And, she'd hurt someone.

Chet called everyday but she had yet to take it. He'd even called Eddie. She should call him back - she did like Chet, but there just wasn't room in her life for a boyfriend, a soon to be ex-husband, and her work with the farm. Chet simply didn't understand her overwhelm and she resented it. Still, she owed him a call.

Savannah rose and brushed the damp leaves off her backside. She wasn't ready to head back to the house but she gotten chilly so she decided to walk and moved toward a more wooded hill that in summer was an impassable collection of brambles. Now dried leaves clung precariously to brittle branches as the fall wind whipped at the vines. Savannah enjoyed the woods, though it could get a bit spooky in the dark. The last month had shown her just how much she loved this land, these cows, this farm. It was more than her home-she had always known that - Morgan Cattle Company was her very essence and the remaining essence of her father, her childhood, and the lives of generations past. She was the caretaker of history now. She felt the souls of those who came before her and sensed her permanence.

Savannah was alone. This farm was now her protector, her parent, and her lover.

Turning out of the thicket, she was shocked into breathlessness by a couple of gunshots so close the boom of the rifles pulsated through her body. Rory dashed off as Savannah strained to see what he'd gone after so quickly. Instinctively she knew what it was; there were hunters in her woods.

"Who's there?" Savannah called out, afraid of the strangers and the impending darkness, but also furious at the injustice of someone hunting the Morgan woods. "There's no hunting here! You damn near shot me!"

She called out again. Advancing boldly toward the sound of the gunshot, the realization that she was an unarmed woman alone in a dark woods began to take root.

Amid rustling a gruff voice answered her. "Hey, lady, we didn't mean to shoot at nobody, you ain't hurt are ya?" Called a man from up above as Savannah noted the hunter's unauthorized tree stand and its metal stair-steeples scarring forever the tall, straight oak. Rory's hackles rose and he emitted a low growl as another man appeared. "There's the dog that ruined our hunt, I guess," he said, as if his problems were important.

"Who the hell are you, and what are you doing hunting this land?"

"Hey, lady, I don't know who you are, but we got permission from the owner to be out here," boomed the man in the tree stand.

"I didn't give permission and I'm the owner. Everyone knows my Dad has never let hunters back here with the cows and besides I'm back here every day checking-"

Descending the tree stand, the man assumed a hostile posture and cut her off. "Hey, not only did we get permission, but we paid to hunt this ground!" growled another scruffy man as he approached. He was short and thick-made and the menacing look in his eyes was hard. The cold, heavy air hung tensely between them. Savannah sensed danger. Still, the word *paid* rang in her ears.

"Who did you pay?"

"The owner, like I said! Troy Howell - he charged us out the ass, too, but said this was virgin woods and some old guy had kicked off that had never let anybody hunt so the place otta be full of deer-"

Savannah bristled. "You need to get off my land. Howell has no authority to let you hunt here."

The man from the tree stand sighed loudly and acted irritated. He was completely garbed in cammo-gear, including a brown and green mottled mask. A chill went up her spine, but she fought the fear down. "Well, its gettin' dark now anyway, but we'll be back, like he said, we done paid to hunt here no matter what you say."

Savannah knew she was out of options and she didn't like the way the short man was edging toward her with what she could vaguely make out as a smirk. She turned and ran back out of the thicket, skidding on the damp slope and tripping over a root. She made it to the four-wheeler, assuming she'd be followed or even attacked. Only the echo of the hunter's cocky laughs followed. While she helplessly sped off they'd made no attempt to leave; her threats had been meaningless. It both intimidated and infuriated her that she should have to fear these powerful intruders on her own farm, a place where moments before she had felt so profoundly peaceful. Her anger grew into white-hot rage by the time she reached the barn.

Troy had done this to her.

He had allowed people to intrude on her farm and endanger her life and the life of her livestock. She had never been so furious. She bumped the barnlot gate lightly with the four-wheeler's grate and pushed through, leaving the gate to bounce on its hinges. She floored it up the drive, threw herself off and plunged into house. Everything was nearly pitch black as she clamored up the stairs. She hadn't yet set foot in her Dad's bedroom and the smell of him, of his aftershave and the detergent on his clothes, filled her nostrils. There was an alive feeling in the room that permeated the darkness with supernatural electricity.

"Don't worry, Dad," she breathed to the energy of the spirit. "I'm going to scare them off just the way you would!" Savannah writhed under the bed, found her Dad's already loaded .22 and grabbed for the box of shells, spilling several as she swept up the weapon and ammo. Only once she was back on the four-wheeler and heading across the pasture again did she notice the raised hair on her arms. Turning back as she drove, she thought she noticed the bedroom lights flicker. She wondered momentarily if she was crazy or if she really was living alone with a ghost.

Savannah took care to approach the woods from an angle where she'd be able to get out quickly. When she was within earshot of the trespassers, she parked, flicked the four-wheelers lights up to high beam, and raised the gun to her shoulder.

"Time to go! Get the hell out of here now because I'm shooting!" She didn't wait for their reply as she fired several rounds into the air. The booming impact on the silent forest was profound. She even managed to bring down a couple of small limbs.

"Hey! That crazy chick's shootin' at us!" one man yelled amid a mad scramble to gather up their gear.

Emboldened, Savannah fired off two more and reloaded.

"Hey! Cut it out!" yelled the other man, his once-mocking voice filled with genuine fear. "That ain't funny. We's going! Quit your damn shootin'!"

Only when Savannah heard an old diesel engine fire did she quit. Then she dialed 911 telling the dispatcher that she thought were two drunks driving an old diesel truck, probably with smoke stacks on the top and straight pipes. That part, of course, was just a guess.

———————— ◆ ————————

Savannah was sitting cross-legged in her Dad's overstuffed chair going over receipts and attempting to balance the checkbook. Her most recent tractor and hay bale moving lesson hadn't gone so well since Eddie wasn't patient and she was not a natural with mechanics. The experience proved just how incompetent she really was. True, she did *eventually* put the round bales, albeit with Eddie's intervention to prevent the disaster of getting stuck or flipping the tractor on a hillside. Frankly, she was shook up. The cows would need hay again in four days and the ordeal would be repeated every week until at least May 1st. Savannah dreaded it and returned to the house at noon dispassionate about everything.

She just felt low.

To add to her concerns, she'd been caught off guard when the mail lady brought a stack of overdrafts; the bank account she'd used in Louisville for the supplies, hotel and fuel hadn't been able to cover it. Savannah had never known her dad not to have enough money for everything, so again, ashamed of herself for not having the foresight to check the finances, Savannah realized she was responsible now and had to be a manager not the daughter of one. A massive feed bill would be coming due, she was overdrawn at the bank and what money she had left on the credit line had to last until she got home from selling heifers in the Denver sale, but it would be February before that sale was settled! Her last paycheck from her 'town job' had come and gone two weeks before and now her only income was the farm, and the farm was overdrawn.

She was so engaged in the books that she jumped at Rory's sudden bark. The dog's hackles rose as he bounded from the kitchen rug to the front door. Savannah was instantly nervous.

Had the trespasser's come back?

Hearing a key attempt to turn the lock, Savannah knew instantly that it was Troy; she'd changed the locks the morning after the choking incident. He evidently still didn't know he wasn't welcome.

Savannah now kept the gun by the office door and she grabbed it. While she didn't intend to shoot Troy, she didn't plan on getting beat up either. Being that he had to be furious about the hunter's, there was bound to be an argument.

Savannah approached the door. "Troy, go home. I've got a restraining order on you and you know it. Get out of here before I call the cops again." She said evenly.

"Restraining order be damned! I've got to talk to you, you raving idiot! Those two guys you shot at and got thrown in jail weren't just any thugs off the street-you have no idea what you've cost me!" Troy exclaimed, beating on the door like an angry child put to bed without dinner. "I'd be safer in jail!"

"Not my problem! You let those bastards hunt on my property where there are cows and -" Troy made her so mad that Savannah's mouth went dry and her voice literally gave out for the heaving of her chest.

"You can cuss me all you want, but we've now got bigger problems than you think. Now, I need to talk to you about money, so let me in!"

"The last time you set foot in this house, you tried to choke me. Get the hell out of here and don't ever let anyone hunt MY property again!" Savannah screamed at Troy, her voice shrill. She felt her emotions shifting out of control again. Abruptly, she charged up the stairs to her room, flung open the window that overlooked the driveway and sat in the sill, one leg perched on the roof, the rifle across her lap.

"We are getting divorced, Troy! It's over!"

Troy was confused by her superior position. "Savvy, what the-"

But his words were drowned out the gun's boom in the air above him. "GET OUT!"

A stunned Troy was sufficiently afraid. Cussing, he scrambled to his truck and took his leave.

Savannah looked out into the night sky.

I'm getting pretty handy with this thing.

~ NINE ~

Holiday gifts

It was an unseasonably cold December, so like many mornings, Savannah was curled up in her Dad's office with a large fire going. It would be a thin trip to Denver with what money was left in her cattle account. She'd contemplated getting a job, but with the trip to the Denver show coming up and cows to manager, she couldn't imagine being tied to a schedule. Savannah had always loved Christmas, but this year the holiday and all its meaning were dead to her. She hated being so down during the holiday season and if it wasn't for constant companionship of Eddie she might have lost her mind with grief and stress. Savannah's recent realization was a painful one. She'd been enjoying all the fun and romanticism of the farm without ever fretting over bills and management. Now, it was bracing to learn Harlan wasn't as well off as she'd always assumed. Savannah had built a budget and she was pretty certain that she could scrimp by until after Denver, but the budget included maxing out her own credit card and even then she would still need winter income after January.

Leafing through the desk, Savannah happened upon the previous year's Denver sale catalog. Their heifers averaged over $4,000 each, a strong showing. Suddenly, Savannah was struck with a thought. She had more heifers in the barn lot than were already committed to the sale because she'd planned on keeping them back in the herd. But, with 65 cows already, she didn't need the increase in numbers, what she needed was an increase in cash flow. Savannah glanced at the desk calendar; it just over 30 days until the sale. She was cutting it close, but she grabbed the phone.

"Drake Jones Sale Management," began a drawling Oklahoma accent.

"Hi, Drake. Savannah Morgan, Harlan Morgan's daughter-I wanted to talk with you about our Denver sale consignments."

"Oh, Savannah, yes. I was awful sorry to hear of your Daddy's passing this fall. Good man he was,"

"Yes, he was. Thank you."

"I assume you're calling to remove your cattle from the sale. I completely understand if this is just too much for you," Drake said. Savannah heard him take a long pull on a cigarette, which in addition to decades of auctioneering, aided in the gravelly nature of his voice.

"On the contrary, Drake. I'm staying in the sale. I was actually calling to see about adding a few more head."

"Oh, I'm real glad you're gonna participate. That's great news. Your cattle averaged real well last year as I recall. But, ah, of course, it's just a little late to be calling about adding any more consignments. I closed it at the end of November. Should have closed at Louisville, but you know how people are-" Savannah cut him off.

"Well, I was hoping you'd be willing to make an exception, Drake, and I sure would appreciate it, you having already said our cattle averaged so well last year," Savannah knew Drake was hesitating, so she pushed on. "In fact, looking back over the catalog, it looks like the Morgan Cattle Company stock averaged about $500 more than the next group of three out there. Surely, you'd like to make a little more money, right? I'd just like to add one more pen of three."

"Three more! Oh, well I can't think we'd do that," chortled Drake as he breathed out smoke, as if choking on Savannah's suggestion. "I would love to help you out, but you know, the catalog is about ready to go to print-"

Savannah again interceded before the Okie could object further. "Well, like you said, my Dad was a good man and I'm now just here with this farm to support," she paused and then went in for the kill. "You and he judged livestock together in junior college, didn't you? He sure thought a lot of you, Drake," Savannah added, pulling out the sympathy card and playing it.

Drake inhaled loudly again and breathed out before he spoke. She'd trapped him. It would get around that he hadn't helped her out if he said no. "Well, as a matter of fact, I hadn't sent the pictures off to the printers yet, so the catalog isn't completely done, I'spose. Your heifers are always a good group."

Savannah was triumphant. "Yes, Drake, six head total-all the same cow family. I'll send over the pedigree information this morning. Your fax number still the same?"

Harlan would have been impressed.

———— • ◆ • ————

The Denver show was generally considered the 'Grand Daddy' of all cattle exhibition events. Each year thousands converged on the old stock-yards to sell, show, and display cattle of at least fifteen different breeds. With the Rocky Mountains as the background and the wild weather that ranged from a balmy 70 degrees one day to a blizzard the next, the show's setting not only beautiful, but at times treacherous. Preparing Midwestern cattle for the Denver event was no small task either; climatic changes like the high elevation and dry air could really be a challenge. Still, Savannah loved the way cattle really looked their best at Denver as the cold weather encouraged the thicker, more lustrous hair coat not seen at summer and fall shows. To get cattle right it just took a lot of work, period. Rinsing in the frigid temperatures and spending an hour or more blowing one out made it an arduous task. The fact that Morgan Cattle Company's barn was not heated nor entirely closed meant using 'salamander' fuel-powered heaters to keep warm. She and Eddie were on an every other day routine of rinsing, Eddie regularly complaining since Savannah added three more head to the program.

It was cold, but once she started working, Savannah had warmed up and shed her down-filled coat. She was now clad in a puff vest and small cap but even under the bright lights of the show barn, her hands hadn't warmed up enough to remove her gloves.

"Damn, it's cold this year," Eddie complained as he led up a dripping wet heifer and attempted to tie her in. The 700-pound calf from the newly added group was only green-broke and had not yet conceded to having Eddie tie her head up. She gave a discontented snort that sent a puff of fluffy white breath and clingy slobber shooting into the frigid air as she balked and bashed Eddie against the side of the barn.

"Hold still, Rip!" Eddie grumbled. He regained his footing and shoved the wide-eyed calf against another heifer, finally getting her tied. "Watch this one," he said, wiping the calf's spit off the side of his down jacket, "She's not above throwing a kick. I swear you picked the wildest snides in the pasture to break right before Denver. Damn it!" he swore again and ambled over to the cooler where Savannah had stored a 12- pack for their afternoon consumption-no ice needed. Eddie popped the bottled Coors Light, tossing the cap absently back into the cooler. He continued with his complaints as Savannah immediately began blowing out.

"Only good thing about getting ready for Denver is thinking about the red beers we'll drink in the yards." Eddie said wistfully.

He apparently didn't require follow up because when Savannah turned again he had ambled back to the wash rack leaving her alone with her thoughts. She generally liked blowing out since over the hum of the blower and the loud whooshing sound of the heater it was hard to hear much else leaving her mind free to wander. She'd been a little less stressed since she'd called Drake Jones and added another pen of three to the sale; at least she would come home with presumably double the money. She'd been living lean, keeping Eddie paid but not spending on much else besides feed. She had to admit that it annoyed her to curtail her previously generous spending habits. She had spoiled herself between her own great salary and limited personal expenses and the fact that her parents had entirely bank-rolled the farm. Since college, she'd acquired about everything she wanted from a nice starter wine collection, to great clothes, to nice dinners out in Indianapolis. In quitting her job and taking over the farm, she neither needed more clothes nor were there clients to wine and dine; it was just she and the cows now. And Eddie.

She hoped it was what she really wanted.

Some days she was just angry.

Suddenly, the heifer balked indicating Eddie's approach. Instead of leading another calf, he carried a long rectangular box.

"What's that?"

"Hell if I know. UPS man just drove it all the way out the barn. Said it was perishable and better not leave it on the porch. It's for you," Eddie quipped, stating the obvious.

Savannah turned off the blower hose and removed her gloves. "Got a knife?" Like any farmer, Eddie immediately produced the desired article.

Savannah had never received such a strange looking package and an irrational fear that Troy was sending a mail bomb fluttered into her mind. Then the return address caught her eye:

Sweetheart's Flower Shop, Carthage, Nebraska

"Oh, no," Savannah whispered.

"Who the hell would it be from?" Eddie asked, irritated and perplexed. He just wanted to be done for the day and the package was holding him up.

Savannah opened the lid to reveal an enormous bouquet of red roses tied with a mass of festive holiday ribbon. A card in a red envelope sat on top.

Dear Savannah,

I want to say I'm sorry. I've pushed you too hard and you just reacted as anyone would. I know there is a shot for us and I'll be more patient. I'm headed to Ohio to pick up some stock for Denver in a few days. Could we meet for a drink or dinner, no strings attached?

Call me.

Love, Chet

"Who the hell sent those? Was it that Tripp Crothers son-of-a-"

"Huh! Definitely not Tripp," Savannah winced at memories of the Texan. "They're from Chet, poor thing, he wants to get together. I don't know if that is a good idea."

"Did he send you a plane ticket to Nebraska, too?" Eddie growled feeling the pit of his stomach knot and pitch with jealousy.

"No. He says he's coming by on his way to Ohio. He wants to meet for a drink," Savannah said, oblivious to Eddie's pain. "I had better call him off," Savannah added with a sigh. The thought of Chet's warmth and kindness sounded so appealing, but she'd vowed not to use the man for her own desperate need for affection again.

As the next few days blended together, every evening Savannah was exhausted and ready just to be alone. Tonight she was looking forward to a hot bath and a glass of pinot noir. It occurred to her that the next day was Christmas Eve.

Reveling in the bath, the divine Pinot, and the luxury of finally warming up, she was startled by Rory's barking. Then, seeing shadows and lights flash off the bathroom walls she realized someone was pulling in. She leapt out of the tub, descended the stairs and picked up the .22 from beside the front door. Rory was barking wildly at the intrusion as Savannah, dripping wet and clad only in porch light and a bathrobe, stepped outside, gun first.

"Don't shoot! I come in peace!"

It was Chet.

———————— •◆• ————————

"Are you gonna invite me in or freeze yourself to death?" Chet joked convivially as he approached Savannah and shyly handed her yet another bouquet.

They stepped into the house, Savannah self-conscious of being without makeup and still surprised to see Chet at 10:00 on a snowy night. "I know it's probably an intrusion, but I had to see you Savannah," Chet admitted as he removed his ball cap and coat. "Actually, I had already 'mapquested' your place before I left Nebraska," Chet answered in response to Savannah's unasked question about how he found the farm. "The damn thing is pretty accurate, though the snow made it a little hard to see signs, but I've driven in worse on the way to Denver!" he joked, then his face turned serious

"My God you're gorgeous without make-up. I've never seen you like that before," he said as if they're relationship had been a long one and she'd done something new. Before Savannah could object, Chet touched her

100

faced and leaned in to kiss her. Savannah stiffened only momentarily then yielded to Chet's soft strength and his gentle, warm kiss.

"I've missed you," he murmured.

By the time she'd dried off and put on a sweater and pants, Chet had taken a beer from the fridge and was sitting on the couch, his boots neatly placed by the back door.

"It's almost Christmas-how is it that you're out here now?"

"Well, we get time off for a couple days at Christmas, so I volunteered to take the drive to Ohio and get the heifers we're supposed to haul to Denver," Chet said with a sheepish grin. "I thought maybe you'd be lonely this year and the thought made me sad."

Savannah wanted to be mad, she wanted to tell him to leave, but Chet was so, well, comfortable. Sitting down next to him, they settled into a comfortable conversation that lasted until almost four o'clock in the morning.

———————— • ◆ • ————————

It was after 9:00 when Savannah heard stirring in the kitchen. The sight of a single long stemmed rose placed beside her on the bed brought Chet's presence back to reality.

He came into my room and I didn't even know it?

Savannah flopped back against the pillows.

How am I going to get out of this one?

Chet was clearly still set on a relationship and now he was in her house. Savannah rubbed her eyes, feeling a headache coming on from lack of caffeine.

She entered the kitchen to see Chet, handsomely clad only in boxer shorts, pouring over an omelet with the intensity of an orchestra conductor. Savannah actually startled him. The kitchen was strewn with pots and pans and fresh coffee was brewing. The living room couch where he had slept was neatly remade, the blankets folded on the ottoman. Chet had obviously been up for a while.

"Hey! I was almost done and I was going to surprise you with breakfast in bed. I'm sorry I woke you," Chet approached her with a kiss that Savannah accepted absently. She was in a state of shock; Chet had overtaken her home and acted as though he was her long lost husband. "I saw Eddie, he said he'd go ahead and do chores since you're sleeping in and I told him great, I'd have coffee for him when he was done. Nice of him to do that for you."

"Eddie's here?"

Oh Boy.

"You must have needed the sleep! Anyway, Eddie's not here. He was outside for about a half hour and left. He didn't come in for coffee. I think he's got a thing for you and was a little uncomfortable with my being here." Chet flipped the omelet and reached into her cupboard for a plate.

"All ready for breakfast sleepy head?" he asked with the sweetest smile Savannah had ever seen.

"Chet, I honestly don't know what to say. This isn't exactly what I had in mind. Last night, I know we kissed, but we can't, I mean, you can't just -" Chet was spared Savannah's rejection by the sight of Jessica's lovely face appearing in the backdoor window. As she wiped away the condensation, her eyes widened to the size of fifty-cent pieces.

Oh my God.

Chet said simply: "Wow, I hope you have enough eggs to feed everybody!"

Savannah hoped that she might die at any moment but no such luck befell her as Jessica stepped inside.

"Darling, I was so worried that you'd be lonely this Christmas so I thought I'd surprise you," said Jessica as she brazenly enjoyed a long perusal of Chet's lean torso and tight belly. "I can see now that you're not lonely at all!"

———————— •◆• ————————

Jessica inviting Chet to stay on for Christmas only confounded the day that Savannah thought could not have gotten any worse. At first, Savannah thought she was dreaming, hungover, drunk, or that her mother had just been mesmerized by Chet's hard body before he skittered upstairs to get dressed. Why else would her mother - the woman who had always seemed so sexless - who had always held Savannah to such high moral standards - invite a strange man to stay with her daughter while said daughter was still married? Savannah was incredulous. Chet made good omelets, but surely not good enough to convince Jessica Morgan that shacking up with her married daughter was a good idea!

Well, he's staying on the couch! Savannah was sure of that.

By evening, Chet had been with her all day, helped with chores and dinner. Now, he sat beside her on the couch as they watched TV with Jessica like a ready-made family.

"Savannah, you haven't really done much with the place yet," Jessica was saying as Savannah was trying not to let Chet get too close to her; he wasn't her boyfriend and she wished he wouldn't act like it.

"Well, Mom, I haven't had the time. I've been swamped with all of the chores, and getting ready for Denver and then there was Louisville, and I-" Jessica cut her off as she shot an examining look at Chet.

"Well, maybe your handsome friend here can help out with all that work. I know how you cowboys operate, always passing through for a time. So how long are you staying?"

Chet smiled, knowing that for some reason he had made a friend out of Jessica Morgan. "Oh, I've got to get to Ohio by the 29th to pick up some stock that our boss wants shown in Denver. Then, it's straight back to the ranch to get the rest of the tack and crew and head farther west," he said casually.

"Well, there you go, Savannah. You've got yourself some cowboy help for a few days so you and I can go shop a bit. Your father is gone and its time you made this place more your home."

Savannah started to object on financial grounds, but Jessica beat her to the punch.

"I'll buy, Lord knows the money is probably getting pretty tight since you've quit your job. It was always my career that bankrolled the cattle operation, of course. Chet, you don't mind, do you?" Jessica said, flashing the young cowboy a gorgeous smile and tapping the lip of her wine glass.

"Yes, Ma'am! I can stay, that is if Savannah would like my company," Chet said happily, jumping up before Savannah could shoot him down. "Jessica, more Cabernet?"

"Absolutely. You're a darling!"

Chet scampered to the kitchen, out of earshot.

"Savannah, what are you saving yourself for? He's a doll; I'd quit being such a prude if I were you. "

A stunned Savannah could think of no reply.

The third holiday surprise rolled up a silver BMW on Christmas Day. Out of a glittering sedan sprang her attorney, Roland Madsen, bearing an armload of gifts. Savannah recalled that he mentioned 'stopping by' over the holidays, but she hadn't taken that to mean that he'd be there for Christmas dinner! Savannah was irritated that her mother would force them to be on the spot on a holiday and she was more than a little embarrassed about what her father's long time attorney would think of her having Chet around-especially when Mr. Madsen was attempting to handle her divorce!

"Savannah!" Roland Madsen exclaimed as he approached the house, his silver hair billowing around him, his slightly ruddy face absolutely beaming. He paused and awkwardly gave Savannah a kiss on the cheek. "I probably owe you an apology," he began casting a wayward glace at Jessica. "Your mother can be a bit persuasive. I am going to assume from your expression that you had no idea that I'd be by today. I know it must be so difficult for you this Christmas," he said, smiling with genuine kindness. "No more Mr. Madsen, call me Roland, okay?"

"Oh Roland, you don't need to apologize! It's so nice to have you here," Jessica's demeanor changed from cool elegance to near giddiness as her voice oozed with an unmistakable flirtatiousness.

The surprises just keep coming, Savannah mused.

Roland hugged her mother and then kissed her on the cheek. "Jessica, you are resplendent and ravishing, as always," he said, with obvious affection.

"Yes, I invited him after I got here and saw that you had a guest. I thought it might round out the conversation if we had two gentleman at dinner," Jessica suggested.

Unbelievable, Savannah thought again.

Odd as it was, the evening passed pleasantly. Roland was nothing short of wonderful company and his gifts were not only extravagant, but completely appropriate, no doubt totally coached by Jessica's perfect suggestions. For all his kindness, Savannah still wished the man hadn't come. Being the first Christmas without her Dad, Savannah felt tears well up whenever Harlan was mentioned and she cried outright when Roland offered a toast to her Dad at dinner. Savannah was absolutely appalled at the way her mother flirted with Roland and even though he tried to act like he wasn't affected by it, it was clear that he enjoyed the attention from the beautiful woman. Her parents may have been separated before Harlan died, but Jessica had taken it too far. Whatever was going on between them was neither discussed nor explained to Savannah, which was fine; she had no stomach for it whatsoever.

The day after Christmas the two women went shopping and Savannah was glad that the time with her mother had at least been fun.

They discussed Savannah and Troy's divorce, though she left out the violence that had gotten nearly out of hand. Her mother would *faint* if she knew she'd actually shot at the jerk. When Jessica apologized about inviting Madsen to dinner, saying she realized it had been inconsiderate, Savannah considered asking if the two were in a relationship, but she held off. Jessica had already said they were old friends, so Savannah left it at that. If there was more to the story, she frankly didn't want to deal with it.

Gratefully, most of the time Jessica prattled on and on about redecorating and spent a near fortune buying things for Savannah to upgrade the old home place. She regarded the heap of materials as projects she could never imagine finishing, but it kept Jessica entertained nonetheless. In the evening, Jessica treated she and Chet to a fine dinner out downtown.

Frankly, Savannah was glad to see her mother go. The holiday had been the oddest and the most difficult in her life. Departure for Denver was less than seven days away, so she felt urgent about getting back to the barn. While she'd been shopping, Chet was left to fend for himself, though he seemed not to mind working on cattle that weren't his own. Savannah deeply appreciated his help; he was a far better hand than Eddie and the stock looked exceptional the way Chet had clipped their tops, hips, and leg hair.

Each evening as the early dark of winter spread its chilly gloom across the barren pastures, she Eddie, Chet went to Billy's bar for supper.

Each night she made Chet sleep on the couch.

When Chet began to profess his love to Savannah over breakfast one morning, she broke it to him as straight saying that while she was enjoying their time together, she was in no way ready for a relationship. She went on to tell him that she wasn't serious about him and though she liked and respected him, she wasn't in love with him. Then she gave him the option to go with no hard feelings. Figuring that Chet would be furious and brokenhearted, Savannah expected him to leave. Instead, he told her he appreciated her honesty.

Wishing it wasn't so unfair to Chet, Savannah acknowledged that she'd still had a lot of fun with him.

While Savannah and Chet were having a good time, there was one person at Morgan Cattle Company who was not enjoying the holiday week.

Eddie was so disgusted that he'd rather vomit than work with Savannah and he was close to telling her so. He'd been one-upped by Chet's talents with the shears and everything else. Savannah had even asked Chet to take her to the sale barn so she could sell a few fat steers for Denver travel money, a chore Eddie had already promised he would do. Eddied was just hooking up the truck and trailer when Chet informed him that he could stay back and that he needed to have the stock dry and brushed out when they returned 'home'. Had Eddie been a stronger man, he would have reared back and knocked Chet's smiling block clean off.

That afternoon Chet had the gall to remind Eddie that it was his last night in town and he and Savannah wouldn't be going to Billy's. Eddie bristled, feeling his bitterness grow into a balloon of anger. Without a word, he headed to his truck and away from Savannah Morgan and her 'boyfriend'. He didn't bother to tell Savannah goodbye for the day; Chet could give her any damn story he pleased.

Eddie headed into town for the horse track bar, a dimly light place where blue-green smoke hung in the air and even the mirrors behind the pool table were coated in the same hazy grime that permeated the air and left his lungs tight upon first breath in the lounge. Regular gamblers lined the tables, their eyes glued to noisy, little personal TV's while their hands stayed busy scribbling on their track programs. I

n the gloom of the track lounge, only addicted gamblers and lonely drinkers passed the time on a Sunday evening. Eddie took a seat at a table off by himself and absently flipped on the miniature TV. A dumpy waitress brought him a beer and offered a smudged glass that he waved away. Without glancing up he told her to keep 'em coming; he was planning to get drunk and be too hung over to go out to Morgan Cattle Company in the morning. The last thing he needed to see was Savannah crying over the departure of Chet. That *would* make him vomit.

Eddie was three deep when a pasty white hand sat a beer down on the table.

"Hey, Ed, what's up? My old lady fire your lazy ass?" cackled Troy, who as usual, was laughing at his own joke. He was clearly drunk and feeling surly. Eddie was in no mood and started to get up.

"What's the deal! I bought you a beer, the least you can do is drink it with me," Troy remarked, flopping himself uninvited into the booth.

"Howell, you make even free beer taste bad." Eddie said, rising to leave.

"Quig," Troy said, using the name that he knew Eddie hated. "Come on, you might want to stay seated, I've got a proposition that even a man like you can't turn down." Troy reached for his arm.

"I've had more than enough of your propositions or whatever you want to call them."

Troy made a big show of pulling an envelope out of his jacket and slapping it on the table. "Hey, take a look."

Curiosity piqued, Eddie reached inside and pulled out a small stack of hundreds. Hastily, he shoved the money back.

Troy was unconcerned. "That's a grand, Ed. There's four more in it for you if you'd like to talk. Sit down and that's your money to leave here with either way."

"You steal this or what? I thought you were going broke or something."

Troy guffawed too loudly. "Hell no! I'm on a winning streak-paid up right now and ahead of the game! That money's not hot Ed," Troy said with a sneer. "Sit down," he said again.

Despite himself, Eddie sat as Troy called to the waitress for another round. "You and my woman headed for Denver this week?"

"Your woman! Savannah is divorcing your ass, clue in, will you?" Eddie said inadvertently eyeing the hundred dollar bills as they poked out of the envelope.

"Yeah, the bitch-oh excuse me-you're in love with my wife-thinks she's divorcing me, but I'm not giving up without a fight. What's new with her anyway?"

Eddie started to speak, but hesitated. He was mad at Savannah, but he was no friend of Troy Howell's. "Yeah, we're leaving in a couple of days. Thinking of casing the place and robbing it?"

"Oh, Ed, you are just so ate up with that woman. 'Course, she's got no time for you," Troy remarked, going on without waiting for Eddie's reply. "Here's where the money comes in. I know Savannah thinks that we are going to get a divorce, but I'm not quitting without a little something for my time and trouble. I need to know if my lovely wife opens her legs for anyone and cheats on her dear husband in Denver. My attorney says if I can prove that she's trying to screw me over then maybe I can sue for at least half of the estate in our divorce. So, here we are. You're a man that needs money and I've got money right now. All I need is some kind of proof that Savannah isn't being a good little girl and you get the cash." He pushed the envelope toward Eddie again.

Eddie didn't respond.

"Take this with you, like I said, as insurance. I know a half-ass cowboy like you can surely use five large."

Eddie had heard enough. He stumbled too his feet, a bit unsteady from the beers he'd pounded in a short period of time. "You're a real piece of work, Howell. I ain't helping you."

As he turned to leave he was hit in the back with the envelope, the banded hundreds falling on the grimy floor with a smack.

"Sure you will, Ed. Savannah's bound to wound your pride and you'll be calling me, I guarantee it."

PART III

The Show of all shows

~ TEN ~

Cade Champion

The Ford dually's lights beamed far ahead blasting the landscape's black stillness as the truck roared through the night. It was late and cold; the dash gage read 9 degrees. They were somewhere in Western Kansas or maybe they'd crossed into Colorado, but Savannah couldn't tell, everything had looked alike since Topeka. The pavement was slick as glass and the wind that assaulted the open prairies kept Savannah white-knuckled on the wheel. Despite her nerves, the road's sameness mile after mile still had a lulling effect and she was getting punchy.

Leaning over to switch the Sarah Evan's CD's once again, Savannah nudged Eddie to quiet his constant snoring. She tapped the accelerator a bit, momentarily disrupting the truck's rhythm and jostling Eddie from his uncomfortable-looking slumber on the opposite side of the cab. He shifted, smacked his lips together as his head lolled to the other side and stayed asleep.

Savannah turned up the music and eased the accelerator back up to 75, singing along quietly to *Born to Fly.*

Dawn came on easily, unnoticed at first. It was only when the blooming red rose of the morning sun appeared in the rear view mirror, that she realized she'd been lost in thought, perhaps lost with the ghosts of the past. The terrain had changed little, but up ahead, she finally saw her first glimpse of the distant Rockies.

"Eddie, wake up," Savannah admonished as she nudged Eddie none-to-gently until he shifted. "Hey, we're less than an hour from Harbinger's, we need to talk-come on, wake up!"

Eddie rolled his drowsy eyes shut again.

"Yeah, yeah, alright. We're close, eh?" Eddie stretched out his arms and popped his neck.

"Wow, it's been an easy trip," Savannah mused just to keep Eddie in the conversation. "You know, the ice could have been worse or it could have been a blizzard on this route, but its been easy. I hope this is a good sign for the week."

"Yeah, not too bad, except now we're fifteen-hundred miles from my own bed, which really sucks," Eddie griped and reached for the watered down fountain cola he'd bought somewhere around 1 am.

"No, Eddie, I'm serious. Something about this week just feels right. It is going to be a week to remember."

From around the country outfits converged on the Harbinger Ranch during the three weeks before and after the Denver show making for a place that was not only bustling but also a near-chaos of trucks and trailers pulling in at all hours of the day, everyday. The concept was called a 'layover' similar to the term used in any other travel, but with livestock it meant giving cattle a chance to rest, recuperate, and acclimate themselves to the climate before heading into the fairgrounds. The Harbinger spread was large and well known and being a wealthy real estate mogul owned that ranch, it had deluxe facilities. If you could get the chance to layover at Harbinger's-you took it. Harlan had been friends with Harbinger's herdsman, Gary 'Wolfsie' Wolf for three decades so when Savannah called and asked if she could stall in for a few days, Wolfsie was more than happy to make room.

Upon arrival, Savannah knew only that they'd initially unload their stock in a large trap, allowing the calves to stretch their limbs and go to hay and water while Wolfsie found them stalls wherever was available. As Savannah was leaving the truck, she caught a quick glance at herself in the rearview mirror. She looked haggard and possibly older than she ever had in her life. Her hair was flat and a little greasy from being unwashed for a day and a half and her mascara flaked at the corners of her dreary looking blue eyes.

"Wow, I've got a bad look!" she muttered to herself, grabbing a farm logo hat off the dash and creating hasty ponytail.

Gazing westward as she walked, her feet skidding slightly at first on the crunchy snow, she moved hastily in the early morning briskness. It was a cold 10 degrees but the sun was up now lighting the mountains with shades of lavender, mauve, and magenta. They were glorious. She truly loved the west, its size and vastness appealing to her in a way that she could neither define nor understand. She took a deep, cleansing breath, allowing the icy air to automatically both refresh and tighten her lungs. She was so enamored with the mountains that she was taken aback when she abruptly hit something.

"Oh! I'm so very sorry!" she exclaimed, shocked that she had just struck someone in the torso; she was paying absolutely no attention to where she was going.

Two cowboys paused only momentarily, both totally engrossed in their conversation, their faces bent over coffee thermoses.

"It's okay, no harm done," uttered one guy as the two passed. Savannah was mortified. For only an instant she caught the eye of the taller man. He seemed to be perusing her with an amused smirk. She quickly glanced away.

I don't want anybody seeing me when I look this bad!

Still, she couldn't help holding his eyes for a slight moment; as she turned away, she was sure she saw him wink.

———————— •◆• ————————

The Angus cattle had moved down to Denver just that morning, so Savannah was delighted when Wolfsie invited her to use absolutely primo stalls just off the expensive sale facility. It was a great spot with a heated wash rack and two big traps for her six heifers and Tiara. The stock would be comfortable and uncrowded and they had access to the barn kitchen, bathrooms, and a lounge with couches, tables and a big-screen TV right next door. Savannah loved showing down in the Denver stockyards but she and Eddie almost wished that the show could take place at Harbinger's posh barn. A girl could get soft working in such accommodations.

They set up stalls while some guys Savannah assumed were ranch staffers worked their heifers through the maze of a chute system that eventually let on to their traps. Savannah looked up to watch the cowboys urging the heifers forward with low reassuring voices and noticed again the tall man that she'd bumped into hours before. Pausing to lean on the pitchfork, she watched him. He was tall, a good head taller than most the other guys and his demeanor and voice were noticeable above the group. Despite his thick down coat and snow pants, she could see that his shoulders were broad and his legs long and brawny. This cowboy was a well-built man who commanded a presence all his own, Savannah observed. He appeared older than her, though she couldn't say he looked 'old' or even how much older she would have guessed him. Maybe it was just the way he carried himself. He wore flinty, reflective shades and a close fitting sock hat brandished with a farm logo she didn't recognize. As he moved the calves he was quick to laugh and poke good-natured fun at the shorter guys that he easily dominated. They appeared to look up to him and worked off his cues. He'd traded his coffee thermos for a cold beer which he'd wrapped in an upside down white cotton glove to act as a make shift koozie. Noticing the brew, Savannah glanced at her watch; even with the time chance it was a hair short of 11:00.

Partier, huh, she thought with smirk. *He might be a fun one to get to know.*

"Hey, who's that guy?" she mentioned to Wolfsie as he walked up and asked her if she needed anything else.

"Which one?" Wolfsie asked, removing his stocking cap to scratch his thatch of thick gray hair that had become sweaty from labor despite the chilling cold.

"That tall, bigger one, the one who seems in charge of the other guys. Is he one of your hands?"

"Hell, no, that ain't one of my guys - couldn't afford him and believe me I've tried. I'm surprised you don't know him. He's from back East- Illinois or Indiana or somewhere like that.

That's Cade Champion."

"No, I've never seen him before. Who's he work for?" Savannah asked as she watched the man called Cade Champion bodily block a heifer that tried to turn on him in the narrow alley-all without spilling his beer.

"Come up with the Bow String Ranch out of Texas, he's been show cattle manager there for several years, I 'spose, " Wolfsie said. Without waiting for her response he added: "Maybe that's why you don't know him, his living in Texas and all. 'Course, he might be a bit older than you, he's been around forever seems like. Best show cattle fitter in the country, I expect." Wolfsie finished.

"Really," was all Savannah could manage.

She liked the looks of Cade Champion.

———————— • ◆ • ————————

Later, Savannah left Harbinger's and drove 15 miles to the closest town and motel. She reveled in a much-needed shower and two-hour nap before heading back to a barn to feed the stock. Eddie was staying at the ranch bunk house and she suspected that he'd enjoyed a nap, too, if he hadn't gotten into a card game already.

The day had faded to a soft shade of periwinkle by the time Savannah wheeled back into the ranch. She was pleasantly surprised to see Eddie already making feed pans. The calves were less than patiently waiting so she had no trouble ushering them into stalls were she and Eddie set individually mixed rations before them. She leaned against the gate and watched them eat as Eddie handed her a cold beer. Accepting it, she reached across the fence and rubbed Tiara's crest while the cattle settled in.

"That Cade Champion guy was by the stalls looking for you. Something about he was sorry he bumped into you this morning," Eddie began as he took a healthy swig; it was not his first beer of the day. In fact, short of taking a shower, drinking free Coors Light courtesy of Harbinger Ranch was about all he'd done the last four hours.

Savannah's heart skipped a beat and she literally felt her throat catch in delight. "Oh, uh, okay, I, uh, I don't know that guy, Cade, um, whatever his name is," she stuttered as she threw back a big drink and immediately choked on it.

"Are you okay?" Eddie asked, perplexed. "Well, he knows you, evidently. Wolfsie said he asked all about you today. The last thing you need is that cow fitter hanging around." Eddie said with a sniff.

Savannah was horrified that the tall, masculine man had noticed her looking so disheveled.

At least I am fixed up better now!

"Oh, that's funny. I don't know him, but I think he must be the guy I accidently walked into today," Savannah shared with a self-deprecating laugh. "I was in a hurry with my head in the clouds and I literally just bowled into these two guys on my way to find Wolfsie. He probably thinks I'm a real dork." Savannah said, trying to make light of her thoughts.

"Way to go, Ace," Eddie laughed. "Sounds like a real slick-cat move, just like you'd make, too. Anyway, don't you know that Champion guy? He's fit cattle all over the country but who knows where a guy like that is really from. Anywhere and everywhere, I 'spose," Eddie said, wiping the icy brew from his lips. "Somebody even said he got married, but who the hell knows with those types. Even if he did, it wouldn't matter-you know how those fitters are-always sniffing up any bar skank that comes around showing her boobs off," Eddie said and reached into the cooler for another. "I'd avoid him, he seems pretty arrogant to me."

"Oh, well, I didn't really notice him, Wolfsie just had to tell me he was some kind of big-deal fitter guy."

"Well, you must be the only person in the cattle business that hasn't heard of him. They say Cade Champion is pretty good."

———————— • ◆ •· ————————

Rich paneling the color of cognac covered the lounge walls, a place more like an upscale bar than the totally understated 'cowboy TV hang-out' that Wolfsie had called it. The floors were polished and pictures hung with individual brass lamps showcased the many bull and female champions that money could buy in the show cattle business. Harbinger Ranch had won all that was winnable at least once or twice-Denver, Houston, Ft. Worth, Kansas City, Cow Palace, Louisville, even the Chicago International back before it closed and the Canadian Agribition, too.

People were draped comfortably across couches, grouped in corners, or leaning against the ornately carved bar that took up the entire back wall. An enormous flat screen TV blasted ESPN highlights as a bunch of guys caught up on the NFL playoffs.

Savannah saw Eddie in the group that was enamored with the sports scores and she faltered momentarily about what to do, finally deciding that a Crown and 7-UP would be a good place to start. Her back was to the crowd as she thanked the bustling makeshift bartender for the free cocktail. Taking her first sip, Savannah sensed rather than saw a presence ease in behind her. When she felt a light, but firm touch to the side of her low back, her heart skipped a beat and as she turned, her eyes tilted upward to meet with deepest blue eyes she'd ever encountered. Looking down at her from probably 6"4 and still touching her back, was the man she'd heard was named Cade Champion. His eyes, teasing and attractively crinkled at the corners, appeared to be enjoying a lengthy and patient perusal of her entire body. He stood rooted there as if staring at her without shyness or even politeness was the most comfortable thing he'd done all day. Finally, without disconnecting his eyes from hers he spoke. "I've been waiting to meet you all day, my name's Cade Champion and you're Savannah Morgan," he said, extending a large, surprising attractive hand out to shake. His other hand remained on her back.

Initially taken aback by his personal touch and surprised that he would announce her name, Savannah faltered only momentarily, but quickly she shot back. "Nice to meet you, Cade Champion. Tell me, do you always stalk women so thoroughly before you sneak up behind them at the bar?" she said in her sweetest coquette voice while she offered Cade a pretty, dainty bat of her eyes. Savannah's self confidence was returning and she smiled up at him daring him to do what, she didn't know. But Cade Champion was unimpressed with the show of flirty nonsense from Savannah. His grip had not left her hand, nor had his cobalt blue eyes left hers. Rather, he squeezed her hand even tighter as he reared back, slightly pulling Savannah with him, and stunned her by boldly laughing aloud as if she'd just told the raunchiest joke he'd ever heard.

"I bet batting those gorgeous blue eyes works for you every day, doesn't it Young Lady?" Cade began, thoroughly amused. "Oh, and I'm sure there are a lot of dumbstruck little boys running around just hoping you'll do that eye flutter thing at them again," he said, clearly mocking her as he then attempted a rude imitation of her eye batting, doing something with his expression that resembled a seizure.

Savannah's was astounded at how quickly he'd turned the tables on her and she was irritated that this brazen man had grabbed her arm, possessively held it way too long, and then proceeded to mock her! Her face and were neck flushing from frustration and her heart was slamming with wild palpitations that kept building every second she was near Cade Champion. Raising her chin in defiance, she jerked her arm away and spun around to face the bar, panting slightly.

"Hey Barkeep, she'll have another Crown and 7," Cade Champion said in a smooth, mocking voice as he eased up behind her again and stood way too close to her ear. It was, admittedly, loud in the cowboy lounge, but not so loud that he needed to be close enough for his breath to stir her hair. Savannah tried to inch forward in an attempt to regain her composure, but she ended up cracking her shin on the shiny brass pole that held up the bar top. "Hey, careful now," Cade drawled in a voice that was masculine, distinctively Midwestern, and soft. "I won't bite, so you don't have to try and escape me. If I wanted you that bad I'd have already thrown you over my shoulder and hauled you right out of here."

Savannah turned to face him, intending to flash him a hot angry sneer. She wanted to get mad, but she just couldn't muster it. Instead, she decided to counter his flirtation with her own.

"If you tried to drag me out of here, don't you think I'd fight a bit and cause you an awful lot of trouble?" she began, trying to act cool while stirring her new drink with the tiny red straw. Then she lifted the short, cool glass to her lips for a sip, hoping all the while that it was *she* that unnerved Cade Champion with the little sucking nose she made when the straw entered her mouth. Her eyes gazed at him over the lip of the glass.

Cade was growing warm inside, whether from the beers he'd drunk all afternoon or from the heat created by the darling young woman, he wasn't sure. What he did know was that no man in this room *or on this earth* was going to come between them tonight. Watching her eyes swimming through the liquid haze of the Crown Royal that partially obstructed his view of her lovely, fair-skinned face, Cade knew one thing like he'd never known before - Savannah Morgan was a woman he wanted like no other.

"I am guessing that you'd fight like a wild little panther cat and kick at me with those long, lean legs and maybe even claw at me with those pretty little hands. But you know what," Cade whispered as he leaned in, "I'd really, really like it."

Savannah felt the warm breath from Cade's mouth softly drift across her cheek as she smelled a faint hint of cologne mixed with the comforting scent of barn float up to her nose from somewhere deep in the collar of his starched shirt. Her stomach literally flipped over three of four times and she almost dropped her drink. Cade's face stayed right where it was, his thick lips, half hidden by a neatly clipped goatee, curled upward in a tantalizing grin as his eyes, fixated on hers, dared her to move away.

Is he going to kiss me? Savannah found herself wondering irrationally.

She'd never stayed in this position with a man so long *with out* being kissed.

As if reading her totally inappropriate thoughts, Cade's smile broadened to reveal two neat rows of teeth and the tip of his tongue. "Have you ever been kissed by a 36-year-old-man?"

Savannah had to move or she was afraid she would fall when her disloyal knees failed her completely.

This man is completely unacceptable!

Savannah had to think fast to compose herself. Leaving the situation was her only option.

She straightened and looked forward, pulling herself to her full height. "Mr. Champion. I am 24-years-old, what would I want with a middle-aged man like you?"

With that, she grabbed up her cocktail so swiftly that some of it sloshed over the side and wet the bar. Then she strode away to the sound of Cade's laughter while she physically felt the heat of his stare send prickles up and down her spine.

———————•◆•———————

It was less than a half hour before her next encounter with Cade Champion. And even though she didn't want to show it, Savannah was thrilled when he sat down next to her at a table of several guys Savannah knew only vaguely. One of the men was a steer trader from New Mexico that bought and sold club calves throughout the Southwest. He and Savannah were pretending to arm wrestle when Cade strolled up. He laid a broad hand across Savannah's straining shoulder blades. "Lonnie Ringo, are you trying to steal my woman? I ought to kick your skinny ass all the way back to the pueblo for messing with her!"

Lonnie immediately dropped Savannah's hand, a move that would have caused her to slump forward if Cade's fingers hadn't dug in slightly and held her up. He hadn't heard Cade was seeing the cute little Indiana girl, but there was no reason to tick off a guy like Champion.

"Hey, Buddy," Lonnie began, looking around shiftily. I'd buy you a drink, but they're free anyway, ya know? I ain't messing with ya'll's girl. She and I was just hanging 'round 'til you got back, that's all," he added standing up and going to refill Cade's beer as if he'd suggested it.

"What was that all about?" Savannah quipped, flipping her long hair over her shoulder. She'd had half an hour to steal glances at Cade from across the room and get just slightly drunk on Crown and 7's. She felt her control return. She loved it that he was back.

"Hey, I'm not the kind of guy to let a good thing go when I see one and when you ran off like that from that bar I got a little sad and wanted to come looking for you."

"A guy like you sad? Texan steer jocks get all the chicks. You surely don't need me to stroke your ego." Savannah said, pleased with her snotty remark.

Cade Champion was not pleased, however. He had always resented the implication that he was just like a lot of guys who were players and cheaters. He'd been around the block, but he wasn't that type, though, before now he hadn't ever really tried to change that reputation. Suddenly, it became important that Savannah Morgan not think that of him.

"I'm no Tripp Crothers and I'm no Texan, either," Cade began, his full, dark brows furrowing in mild irritation as his broad forehead knotted in the center giving him a foreboding look. Savannah was stung by the Tripp Crothers remark.

Surely that incident in Louisville hadn't made it already to Denver...

"Like you, I'm from back East and I just happen to work in Texas," Cade sniffed. "And yes, I do know that most of the guys that have that kind of reputation have earned it."

Savannah could see that he was miffed, though she had no idea why he'd care what she thought of his behavior. Still she decided to back off the cute insults, at least for the time being. "Would you like to sit down, Cade Champion?"

"I would love to sit down with you, Young Lady."

Though the inevitable had just happened, neither Cade nor Savannah was aware of it yet, but they were aware of a keen attraction that pulled them into a conversation that lasted nearly three hours before Savannah announced she needed to excuse herself. Standing, she trembled slightly on wobbly feet causing her hand to drape over Cade's shoulder as she rose. Cade touched her hand with his palm, holding it a moment.

"Easy there, Party Girl," Cade said gently. All he wanted to do was envelope Savannah Morgan in his arms and kiss the sass right out of her. "Need me to haul you to the restroom?"

"Me? Of course not, Cade," Savannah cooed while she forcibly willed her body to right itself.

I'm acting like a teenager!

"I probably need to get away from you for awhile in case people actually believe the lies you've been filling Lonnie Ringo with about me being your woman! As if!"

Savannah attempted to stalk off toward the restroom. Musing a few moments in the stall she tried to compose herself again. She couldn't believe her attraction to Cade.

There is no way he is as hot as I think he is! And, I'm letting him mock me while I take it and fawn all over him!

"I've got to pull it together!" she said aloud. Getting some icy cold Colorado mountain air was just what she needed.

Emerging from the restroom, Cade watched Savannah head straight for the side door that led to the barn and cattle stalls. Cade cussed slightly under his breath. "Damn it! She didn't even bother to take a jacket." He grabbed his down coat and without the good sense to wait a few minutes, followed the unsuspecting Savannah outside.

Looking for something to do in an effort to sober up, Savannah stepped into the dimly lit tack area and searched around for a salt block. The heifers were all sitting peaceably in various spots nestled down into the insulating snow, but she'd noticed one of the girls licking, a sign that maybe she needed mineral. Emerging from the stall, she didn't notice Cade Champion shadowed against the barn's eve until a firm hand grabbed her arm and pulled her towards him.

"I asked you once already, but you didn't answer, Savannah," Cade said, his voice husky. "Have you ever been kissed by an older man?"

"Cade! You scared me to death!" Savannah said nearly dropping the salt block she held between them. "I didn't see you there," she averted her eyes so he couldn't see them. Her heart was pounding so hard it physically hurt and her head was swimming at the sight of his chiseled face so close to hers in the dim lights of the barn.

He so was masculine and firm and near....

"Set that down, Savannah, because I am going to kiss you now. I think I've waited long enough tonight."

With one hand, Cade easily slid the 10-pound block from Savannah's grasp and somehow, without loosing the locked gaze he had on her eyes, he set it to the ground. As Cade straightened, Savannah turned and moved toward one of the stalls, again averting her eyes from Cade's intense, locking glance.

Cade was not daunted.

"You know, I may just go farther than kissing you, I may kiss you, love you, and make you my wife all before we leave Denver. What do you think of that Young Lady?" he said advancing on her slowly, deliberately, as if chasing cowering prey into a dark, inescapable corner.

Cade took her in his arms, then lifted one hand to her chin, turning it upward to bridge the four-inch gap in their heights. "Would you like to marry me Savannah Morgan?" he said with a teasing lilt to his soft, earthy voice.

Savannah didn't speak. She could not speak. She just met his eyes unfalteringly and gazed into something she knew she would never forget as long as she lived. Cade moved closer, pressing his firm chest upon hers, igniting fires within both of them that neither was prepared to believe.

"No answer, huh? Well, I'm patient. Tonight I'll just settle for a kiss."

Cade's dark head bent over Savannah's and as his mouth tasted hers for the very first time, he felt her velvety blonde hair brush his cheeks as the draft stirred the tendrils. At first slightly shy, then suddenly hungry for more, Savannah's lips parted widely and she stunned herself by gripping the back of his starched shirt as he firmly held the entire side of her jaw in one hand, the small of her back in the other. The heat of their kissing contrasted sharply with the frigid evening and the nauseating warmth of the cowboy lounge. Cade moaned and learned into Savannah as his craving for her soft lips was eagerly fulfilled. He pushed her against the boards of the wooden stall and Savannah felt the weight of his body pressing down on her in earnest as their kiss deepened and their hearts melded together for the first time...

~ ELEVEN ~

MOVING FAST

Savannah slept deeply for the first two hours of the short night, but after the alcohol wore off, she was awake and thinking of Cade Champion. Laying there, practically nauseous from the butterflies bouncing in her stomach, she was consumed with his eyes, his smile, his firm hands gripping her, the kiss they'd shared. *Surely* he wasn't as awe-inspiring as she'd thought last night. He was cute, no -

Cade Champion was dead sexy.

Yes, but that doesn't mean I have to fall all over him!

This was the first day in Denver, no, in Colorado! She hadn't even gotten to Denver yet! There was no reason for her to repeat her Louisville behavior- that was for certain.

It must have been the thin air, she thought, even as reminders of his scent, his naughty grin, and his teasing remarks cluttered her mind.

By 7:30 a.m. she was mixing feed against the stoic backdrop of the Rockies, the lavender morning light brightening to crystal blue with every passing moment.

"Early riser, even with a hangover-I like that," came a familiar voice from behind. Savannah was in a rather compromising position being bent forward while dumping out feed. Cade's grin made it obvious that he'd enjoyed watching her backside splayed out as she stooped. "Ya look good, too," he said, cocky as ever, as he stepped into the stall and left little room between Savannah and the door. He had that just-showered fresh, soapy smell and at close range, Savannah could even whiff the minty toothpaste emanating from his mouth. The hint of cologne that floated up headily from the collar of his starched shirt caused Savannah's stomach to flip with desire. He looked wide-awake, as if yesterday's libations hadn't bothered him at all.

Is he going to kiss me again in broad daylight? Savannah's irrational mind screamed.

"Think about me last night?" Cade asked, flashing a beguiling smile that implied he knew exactly that she *was totally* consumed with thoughts of him. She flushed instantly.

"Actually, no. But it was fun while it lasted, so thanks for the mash," Savannah shot back, forcibly brushing past the broad chest that blocked her exit. She needed to get away from him so she could stand.

What does this man do to balance?

"Mash! That's an immature little college-girl word!" Cade guffawed, as though she'd said something hilarious. He was going to enjoy falling in love with Savannah Morgan; she had lots of pep and was witty, too.

"I'll check on you later and make sure you don't need any help. You're herdsman's finally up, I see," noted Cade as he cast a disapproving glance toward Eddie who tottered toward Savannah, barely one eye open.

"What's up, Ed? Ya didn't let those outlaws from Kansas rob you blind at cards last night, did ya?" Cade asked, his mocking grin far too spry for Eddie's lack of early morning charm.

"How'd you hear 'bout that already?" Eddie asked, confused.

Cade laughed boisterously again, a merry laugh that said he could be amused at a funeral. "I hadn't! I was just jokin'- now it's really funny though!" Cade cracked as he shot a smug glance at Savannah.

The man was completely rude!

But Savannah found herself snickering anyway at Eddie's apparent folly with the Kansan card players.

"Hey, Ed, take care of your boss, she's a hottie and guys'll be hittin' on her if you don't watch out," Cade finished with a pat so firm on Eddie slumped shoulders that the shorter man stumbled a step.

Eddie glared angrily as Savannah stifled another smirk at Cade's apparent dominance over any man who was not his immediate equal. "Texan jerk."

"Actually, he's not from Texas. He's -"

"Couldn't care less," was Eddie's retort.

———————— •◆• ————————

Rinsing and blowing out heifers in freezing weather was usually no pleasant task, but Savannah found herself breezing through the cold, grueling work with ease. Certainly, the heated facilities made it easier and she loved working hair, anyway. She was even humming a Sarah Evans song all morning. Eddie, however, was irked but the audacity of Cade Champion, a man who Savannah apparently thought was damn clever with his remarks.

Figures, Eddie thought.

The man probably had every chick North of the Rio Grande smitten with his crooked grin and broad shoulders. Begrudgingly, Eddie recognized that Cade was one of those guys that girls automatically looked at twice, the typical tall, dark, and handsome kind, of course. The last thing he wanted was a fast-talker like Champion hanging around.

But, hang around all day, Cade surely did. By noon the swarthy cowboy had made occasion to stop by the stalls three or four times. Once, he thought Savannah might want to know something about move-in day down at the Yards. Another time he offered her some nice hay he'd brought up from Texas. Then there was the time he came over and asked Eddie if wanted any help shearing the bellies on the heifers and if they had anyone lined up to buy them yet. Finally, Cade Champion came over just to flirt with Savannah.

Eddie thought the man was a menace but Savannah could not see it. While she giggled and laughed at his stories, she still appeared to keep her distance. Eddie was proud of her for trying to hold him off, but it didn't deter Cade. Eddie noticed the way he stared at Savannah, not looked, but rather *stared* as if he was literally planning to swoop in and kidnap her. Eddie new Savannah was pretty, hell, he'd grown up with her, but he realized maybe he had overlooked the way other guys saw her-as a real hottie fresh on the market. It was now apparent to Eddie that he had underestimated what a pain in the ass it was to have attractive boss. He hadn't even been rid of Chet for two weeks! Now, already there was another cowboy underfoot and they weren't even to Denver yet.

Thoughts of Troy's offer crept into his mind, but he pushed them aside.

———————— ◆ ————————

Cade hadn't said one word to Savannah about the kiss, but she knew he surely must want another the way he flirted with her all day and looked at her with open desire. Maybe older guys don't bring it up in conversation, she mused.

He's practically 40! Was a thought that entered Savannah's mind at one point during her daydreaming. She tried, but every time she looked at Cade, it became impossible to get the thought of kissing him out of her mind. It was, she realized about noon, the kiss of her life. Yes, she had to admit it, while she had no business thinking about him, she just couldn't stop.

Kissing him was phenomenal.

———————— •◆• ————————

By mid-evening she and Eddie were watching football in the cowboy lounge. She was sulking, and knew it. Having not seen Cade in hours, she'd heard that his crew left to take tack down to Denver. It irritated her that he hadn't told her he was leaving.

It irritated her even more that she was irritated.

She knew that was ridiculous. All day she'd been certain that Cade had felt the same overpowering surge of emotion that she felt the night before, too. But, maybe she was wrong; maybe he was just another cowboy. It was starting to annoy her that he had been flirting and coy all day, never mentioning their moment together. It was getting late, nearly 11:00, and Savannah decided she needed to drive to the motel. Rising, she headed for one last stop at the restroom.

Just as Eddie and a few other guys were speculating about how the Bow String crew finagled getting onto the fairgrounds early, Cade strolled in and doffed his drenched parka.

"Damn, that weather's nasty out there!" Cade swore as he ran slender fingers through his thick tawny-colored hair, a move that sent sprinkles of water trailing down his neck. "Sleet, ice, rain!"

"Took us three hours to get back up here!" chimed in one of the crew. "Get me a whiskey."

"Where's Savannah," Cade asked Eddie as his eyes scanned the cowboy lounge. He hoped she was either already at the hotel or at least not out on the roads.

"Just missed her Champion, she went to the hotel."

"Why'd you let her do that, the roads are terrible, she-"

As he started to upbraid Eddie, he saw Savannah leaving. She'd seen him – and ignored him.

"Damn stubborn girl!" Cade swore again, striding after her.

Savannah had already reached her truck by the time Cade caught up.

"Hey! Where you going so fast?" Cade began gently tugging her arm. "Let me drive you back, these roads are awful."

"What do you care?" Savannah quipped, and immediately regretted the juvenile way it sounded. The sleet was dense and freezing cold, matting her hair almost instantly like a soaked shower cap. She tried to recover the dumb comment. "I mean, don't worry about it, I know you've got a lot going on with your stock, too."

Cade's heart warmed to the thought that she'd wondered about him. *So she really is interested in me.*

"Savannah, I meant to tell you we were leaving, I did, but the tack got loaded up and the trailer was ready and I actually didn't expect the weather, so I figured I'd be back about dinner time."

"It's no big deal, Cade."

"It *is* since you wondered where I was. I'm glad you wondered about me," Cade said, sliding closer and pushing her into the truck cab. "Get in, I'm happy to drive you. I'm serious, these windy road are dangerous."

Savannah softened, letting him urge her into the cab. "Why didn't you just call me?"

"I guess I could have stopped at a pay phone."

"Pay phone!" It was Savannah's turn to mock Cade. "It's 2000, Cowboy! I mean call me on your mobile!"

Cade turned the key in the ignition. The diesel took a couple tries to fire, its cold cylinders coughing to life. "I don't have a cell phone. 'Guess I never figured anyone needed to reach me that bad before."

———————— •◆• ————————

"I'll take your truck now and come get you in the morning, is that alright?" Cade asked as he pulled under the hotel's breezeway.

"Yeah, sure, I really appreciate it, Cade," she said, her hand on the door.

He gently grabbed her left wrist, tugging her back toward the center of the cab. She waited for some sexy, taunting remark, but none came. "I know we had a few laughs today, Savannah, but I really want to get to know you better. I was wondering if you'd like to go to dinner with me tomorrow night."

He is asking me on a date!

Savannah's pulse picked up. She hoped Cade couldn't feel it in her wrist.

"I suppose I could, if you're really desperate for a dinner companion."

"Oh, I could find plenty of dinner companions, Savannah. What I want is you."

———————————— •◆• ————————————

Savannah and Cade were seated on the same side of a booth in the local bar where they'd ordered beers and steaks. She was having a wonderful time with Cade, but just couldn't get over how much he stared at her. As if reading her mind once again, Cade put down his knife and fork and leaned closer.

"You know, I might as well come out and say it. You're beautiful, Savannah Morgan. Not cute, not pretty even, just plain gorgeous."

Savannah blushed. Cade had been lavishing her with compliments all evening. She had never met anyone so totally bold. She knew men often found her attractive, but most weren't so obvious about it. Well, Chet had been, but somehow it wasn't the same. It was like she never heard Chet when he praised her looks. Cade's compliment was so different, so much more powerful, that she hardly knew how to react.

Raising her chin she said: "Cade Champion, you're relatively handsome yourself, I suppose."

"Relatively, eh? Do you always kiss relatively handsome men so passionately?" Cade's blue eyes twinkled and he winked at her as he sipped his 32 oz.

"Oh! So we're finally going to talk about it, huh? I was beginning to think you just went around the barn kissing all the girls."

Cade's mood darkened again and he slid a rugged hand across the table grasping Savannah's before she could reach for her beer. "I told you, I don't play those kinds of games. I kissed you like that because I was, no I *am*, interested in you and only you."

"Oh." Was all Savannah could think to say. Cade could be so intense and then so flip all within a moment's time.

"Cheer up, Young Lady. I didn't mean to scare you," Cade said, eyeing her plate. "Hey, you've haven't eaten anything! Try some of these mushrooms and onions, they're delicious!" he said forking over a heap of the veggies as he helped himself to her cheesy potatoes, hungrily devouring them. "Mmmm, these are excellent! 'Can't believe you've left these on your plate!"

Savannah wanted to comment about how odd it was that he be so familiar with her, but the truth was it was just fine if Cade ate the food. Her stomach was flipping so much from his nearness that she didn't dare put anything in it.

"So, how'd you get to the Bow String from the Midwest anyway?" Savannah asked, trying to keep the conversation light.

"Well, that's a long story, I guess. I mean, in my line of work, you work for one guy, then another guy comes calling or the first guy runs outta money and you find yourself looking for another gig, and, well, eventually, you just end up at a place," Cade said.

That wasn't much of an answer.

"Well, what do you do down there? Are you the show cattle manager or the herdsman?"

"Barn bitch."

They both laughed.

"No, I mean it! Do you have any cows of your own?"

"You're awful curious!" Cade chided as he leaned over and gave her neck a long, slow kiss. "Yes, I own a few, you could say, and they're down at the Bow String. Ready to get out of here?"

At the truck, Cade came around and opened her door first, then he pulled her to him.

"Not so fast, Young Lady." They melted together instantly, kissing softly for only a moment before the heat of their attraction fell over them like a veil. Kissing Cade was almost a relief since Savannah had now been anticipating it for a day and a half, an apparent eternity. She caved against the truck's fender as Cade pressed her to him, drowning out the world.

"I wanted to kiss you so badly all day I thought I might just loose control and attack you in broad daylight. We'd better get in the truck." Cade breathed.

Savannah's knees were ridiculously weak again and as she accepted Cade's assistance into the truck cab, her stomach lurched so wildly that her breath was coming in gasps.

What is this man capable of doing to me?

———————— •◆• ————————

Savannah had the disquieting notion that she was deceiving Cade. The night they met it would have seemed random to have announced that she was desperately trying to divorce a man she loathed and since then no convenient time had arisen for her to bring it up. I probably should have been done at supper last night, she reasoned, but she'd been so nervous and then they'd had so much fun that she just couldn't bear to ruin the moment. Still, considering the time they'd already spent together, and the seriousness of her feelings, she had to either tell Cade she wasn't interested in anything long term (at least right now), or tell him she wasn't exactly single. Both options were horrible. She wanted Cade and the overpowering attraction was enough to drive her truly insane, but something told her that he wouldn't approve of her being married and their fooling around. She had to tell Cade eventually, of course, but Savannah convinced herself it could wait until after Denver, until after whatever might be between them had a chance to take root as something real. Cade hadn't asked her about anyone 'back home' nor had he volunteered his marital status, either. So, Savannah decided to take it day by day. For about the millionth time, she wished Troy Howell never existed.

As Savannah's heifers ate in the purple twilight of the day, Cade approached from behind by placing a firm hand on the back of her coat.

"Hey gorgeous!" he chirped happily. "You promised me a date tonight, right?"

"I don't remember talking about that at all, actually," Savannah said coyly, a little shy about his outward affection, but not wanting him to cease.

How could someone so large appear so easily out of thin air? He really is a panther, Savannah thought wantonly.

"Maybe! Oh, it's more than maybe - let me tell you that! There's a group going into town to play pool and drink beer at the place where we ate dinner last night. Will that suffice for you?"

"Do you mean the company or the food?"

"Oh, you think you're cute now, just wait until I get you alone again!" Cade said slyly. Then to Savannah's shock he swatted her swiftly on the rump. "Be ready to go in less than an hour."

Being out with Cade was just as much fun as being alone with him, Savannah was amused to notice. Amazingly, watching him in action and not touching him increased her attraction by the minute. It seemed to her that Cade Champion could probably do anything. He proved to be an avid pool shark and was excellent at darts. As he laughed and chided the guys, it was apparent that everyone knew him.

Cade was a man among boys.

Other guys looked up to him, were intimidated by him, respected him, and feared him. Some quite obviously envied him, others liked drinking with him, and some thought he was a jerk. No matter what, Cade Champion was the man in the room and Savannah knew it would be that way wherever they went.

By eleven o'clock Cade was making their excuses. Considered early by cowboy social standards, it was obvious that Cade and Savannah were leaving together. She could have been embarrassed, but it seemed a moot point. Cade had made it perfectly clear that they were an item and she was not to be approached. She loved the feeling of being *possessed* by him. It was just - hot.

In the hotel parking lot, Cade killed the diesel engine. They sat in silence for a moment before he reached for her hand.

"How do you feel about me coming in for a while?"

"I think that it would be nice, Cade," she said, too formally. Savannah didn't know what would happen if she were actually alone with Cade and the thought was almost frightening. As she watched him slide, lithe as a cat, out his side of the truck, warmth spread across her lower abdomen and butterflies flitted up the sides of her body. What had happened at Louisville was nothing. What Cade Champion's simple presence did to her was absolutely *animal*.

Savannah half expected Cade to attack her in the elevator, but he didn't. When they entered her room, Cade removed his coat and gloves then pushed her oversize down jacket to the floor. As if moved by forces of nature, they came together in an embrace that would have crushed the breath out of most people. Savannah caved against him feeling absolutely lost in the heat of Cade's strong, alluring power. Being together seemed to breathe new life into both of them. They kissed slowly, eagerly, exploring each other.

"Savannah, you are so damned beautiful and you kiss like no one I've ever touched. God, I'm going to fall hard for you," Cade said as he lifted her chin so their eyes met. Savannah wanted to say something back, but didn't, instead, she pushed Cade's hand up the side of her ribs, inciting a moan from Cade so deep she it rumble deep within his barrel chest. "You're going to get what you ask for if you offer it, Young Lady. I'm a grown man, not some 25-year-boy you can play with."

As Cade carried Savannah to her bed, she couldn't articulate what she was after, just that she wanted more, *forever* more of the overwhelming warmth and heat that emanated from Cade's very being and held her in its loving embrace. She was floating high; no man had ever made her feel so weightless, so special, or so beautiful. Cade was incredible.

They kissed for a long while but abruptly Savannah pulled back. Something in her conscious just wouldn't let her go farther with Cade. She had never been so afraid nor desired a man like this in her life. It was so urgent, so immediate and everything about Cade seemed so inexplicably life altering. It wasn't simple, it wasn't just kissing - it was kissing Cade Champion. Being with him was like watching a mentalist move a mountain; there was no explanation to why or how it worked, just that it did. She didn't know why she knew it, but she had to be careful, for both of their hearts.

"Cade, Cade," she murmured against the thick neck that was nuzzling her ear, "I'm, um, could you lean back a minute?"

Cade pulled back, but allowed a sinewy hand to remain against her check. His deep cobalt blue eyes seemed to bore into hers. He seemed completely calm, not irritated at all the way Tripp had been when she pushed him away. "Ready for me to go home, Savannah?"

"It's not that I want you to leave, because I don't. I'm just not sure - I mean, I'm not ready for-"

Cade sat up and ran a hand through his thick sandy brown hair feathering it back with his fingers, a move that caused Savannah a powerful desire to do the same thing. Her stomach flipped over again and her chest tightened.

She never imagined that a man could be that sexy.

Cade seemed to be contemplating something. Savannah was not versed in the ways of men, particularly not 36-year-old bachelors. Finally, Cade reached for her and laid the two of them back on the pillows, side by side.

"Let's talk then," he said.

Afraid he'd somehow figured out about Troy, Savannah bristled slightly. "Uh, about what?"

"Well, let's talk about you and cattle showing. I mean, why are you 2,000 miles away from home with a lazy local hand and seven head?" Cade said in such a matter-of-fact manner that she could hardly believe her own nonsense at showing in Denver. Cade pulled her head across his chest. "I mean, a guy like me, well, I'm here because I have to be. I work for the ranch, they want to win, I make that happen, and I get paid. It's easy for me, but you, beautiful Savannah Morgan in my arms, why have you graced Colorado with your presence?"

"Well, I guess it's about a heifer and the thought that she might win," Savannah began. Then, when Cade neither added more nor endorsed her point, she charged on. "It's about the thought that she is the last of her lineage and that she could have won, no, should have won, but she hasn't yet. Denver is her last chance. I don't know if she'll win here, either, but if I don't try, well, then I've let her down."

Cade breathed out a long, slow breath. He'd been showing cows a long, long time. Though not quite 40, he'd been on the road for 25 years. He was good - damn good - at what it took to win for his clients. But he didn't care about winning anymore.

What he knew was the road. The road meant driving a truck alone all night between the Midwest and Texas or between California and the South East, eating nothing but fast food and guzzling cokes and No Doze to stay awake. The road meant arriving at a show where somebody had already determined who was going to win and what his role would be in getting the right stock fit the right way for the right judge. The road meant lots of beer and plenty of women and rich jerks with more cash than sense, the kind that spent big money and won a show the first time out and then stood around and told you that they'd figured out how 'easy' it was to win a cattle show.

As if they had any idea what it took.

Sometimes it was just about more than Cade could stand. Mostly, the road meant empty victories and lonely Sunday nights eating bagged popcorn and watching cable TV. Showing was a job and it was the only job he'd become qualified to do. It had been so long since he'd heard someone want to win for the sheer, genuine love of an animal that he felt like crying. Savannah was so sincere and naïve. She wanted the win, but she also believed that if she didn't try she'd be cheating Tiara out of the shot that might rightfully have been hers. Cade felt Savannah renew him.

He pulled her closer and kissed her again. Just as she started to kiss back, he stopped. "Savannah, talk to me more. Tell me about your home."

Perplexed at first that Cade would rather talk, she settled in nonetheless. They talked about her farm, her Dad, her boring job, the fumes she was coasting into Denver on, the need to sell the six heifers, and of course, her desperate goal that Tiara could win. Cade listened to her, asked questions, gave her ideas about selling the heifers, and promised he'd do whatever he could to get the Tiara heifer to the Grand Drive. They talked about everything.

Everything but Troy Howell.

———————•◆•———————

Savannah awoke gently, as if she was lazily sleeping in her own bed on a Sunday morning. She felt a strong arm around her mid section and heard Cade's even breathing. Except her boots, she had on all of her clothes.

"Good morning, Gorgeous," Cade mumbled against her ear, his body snugged completely against her backside, shoulder to toes. "Wow. You smell delicious after a few hours of sleep."

"Is it morning, really?"

"Yeah, Pretty Girl, it's about 6:00."

Savannah started to shift and get up, but Cade tightened his grip. "Hey, let's talk a minute."

She giggled. "I thought that's how I got in this compromising position to begin with."

Cade chuckled, too, but remained serious. "I mean it. We're all heading to the Yards today. I don't want to lose whatever it is we've started to build. Tell me you'll be with me this week, Savannah," Cade began, and then, before she could answer he added. "I need to know. Will you be with me this week and try to figure out what comes next for us?"

Savannah's heart skipped. It was amazing to her that Cade was so deliberate, so honest, so loving. She couldn't imagine anything in the world as natural as being with him. "Cade Champion, you've got yourself a deal-for better or worse, I'm yours for the week."

~ TWELVE ~

THE YARDS

Savannah was convinced that the old stockyards was the eighth wonder of the world. Or, at least its mile-high setting was the coolest stage
for a cattle show of all time. Showing or browsing stock in the yards was
considered a not-to-be-missed event for the many showing 'pilgrims' that
converged on Denver once a year to pay homage to the bygone era of cattle
drives and rail cars, of big ranches and wide open spaces. From 'the hill' -
literally a vantage point of clustered buildings and arenas overlooking the
stockyards - one could view acres of cattle. It seemed as if the pens of cattle
stretched all the way to the very base of the majestic purple Rockies that
stood as the backdrop to the Grand Daddy of all livestock shows.

It was good to be in Denver!

Moving in from places all across America, hundreds of trucks and
trailers stopped at the same gate to check in before proceeding. Denver took
check-in seriously; cattle rustling was not just folklore of the old west-peo-
ple still stole high dollar livestock to resell and expensive trucks and trailers were always a target, too. Over the cold grumble of diesel motors, vets

checked health papers, show officials reviewed entry forms, and certified brand inspectors looked out for everything else. Livestock haulers jockeyed for position as close to the front of the half-mile long line as they could-sometimes the wait for check-in could last hours. Though vets, brand inspectors, and show personnel were unyielding, there were always a few of the parking guys that could be encouraged to help you move up a little faster in the line. With beer, whiskey, or even some nice logo trinkets such as a hat, gloves or coffee mug from a famous ranch, you could be on your way through the line in minutes not hours and you could also expect a nice parking spot once you got inside. It was a poorly kept secret, apparently, but Savannah hadn't heard of it until Cade explained why he'd gotten her truck and trailer to breeze through while a line of frowning faces watched her roll through the gates. Harlan certainly would not have stood for that kind of angling, Savannah mused. Cade was nothing if not effective, it seemed. Savannah was more in awe of him by the day. Eddie just scoffed; he didn't have to like the guy, but anyone who could keep them out of the entry gate line was worth at least being nice to for a few hours.

Exhibiting in the Yards meant that stock and owners were outside all day in whatever fickle temperatures Denver experienced in January. Mornings were usually frigid and dry while afternoons ranged from gorgeous sweatshirt and sunglasses weather to miserable, snowy slush. Savannah noted the kaleidoscope of colored little tents and shanties being erected as cattle jocks set up a base camp for the week.

Cattle typically adjusted well to the dry Denver cold and were heavily bedded outside in large pens with straw or wood chip shavings underfoot. During peak times of visitors during the day, the stock would be rinsed, blown out, clipped, and sprayed to a high sheen with products to make their thick winter hair shine. Exhibitors displayed their bulls and females on beds of high quality bark so peers and potential buyers could check them out.

Setting up for Denver was a big job that took a day or better in camp construction alone. Beer and whiskey drinking started early either to ward off the cold or just to add to the fun as exhibitors greeted old friends often not seen since the previous year. From trailers, people unloaded long metal gates that separated one animal from another in the stalls. They set up curtains as backdrops and added elaborate, professionally printed banners to hang above each animal's head proclaiming its pedigree, name, and if the animal was for sale. Large banners brandished with individual farm logos advertised upcoming winter bull sales or semen packages available on new stud bulls. Tack also took up a lot of the display space with casket-sized aluminum boxes stuffed to overflowing with scotch combs, curry combs, fine tooth combs, skip toothed combs, tail combs, blowers, and adhesives and sheens that would be used literally from head to tail. Flyers or brochures were handy at most stalls and some even used electronic screens or laptops to promote events or highlight photos of the donor cows back at home. The worn wooden alleys, once swollen with fat steers bound for Kansas City and Chicago's meat packing districts, were now literally covered from bricked ground to top rail with flyers advertising bull semen to border collies, heifers to cutting horses, and strip clubs to steakhouses.

History, or just the passage of time, had eroded the stockyards with its aging cement catwalks and cobblestone roads. But the mystic of Denver would never be lost among those who loved it; Savannah was one of those who felt in her soul the power of the past and its pull on the present. It was hard not to think about the impact of those who'd gone before in building the cattle industry when you were in the Yards. She was thinking of the past as she gazed at the old Stockyards Exchange Building, an imperceptibly leaning structure of a washed out hue that had once been the hottest ticket in Denver's packing district. Now, while business was still conducted there daily, it was more known for it's annex, The Stockyards Inn, or as everybody called it 'The Yards Bar'. That's where she and Cade would go later tonight and Savannah would show the world that she was with him.

The thought was thrilling, and disconcerting-she wasn't divorced and a lot of people knew her. Macy had called to say that she was flying in tomorrow and Bella's crew was in line waiting to get in. She hadn't told the girls yet about Cade-there hadn't been time-but she was pretty excited to fill them in. And, she was hoping to learn more about Cade from Macy; two guys like Cade Champion and Stetson Rawlings *had* to know each other.

Apparently a mind reader, Cade at that moment placed an invasive but tantalizingly warm hand inside Savannah's coat right above the back of her waistband.

"Is it time to go to the room yet?" he breathed into her ear.

Savannah felt her knees buckle. She turned and met his gaze.

Could he get any hotter?

"No!" she said jumping away as if not interested. "We're got a lot of setting up left to do and all I've seen is you running your mouth," she giggled. It was true; Cade knew *everyone*. People had stopped to talk with him the entire day.

Cade laughed his deep throaty laugh and grabbed her coat, swinging her wildly to him. "I'd like to be running my mouth-all over you."

"Cade! Hush, I don't want Eddie to deal with this yet. Lay off, at least just a little!" Then, thinking of the Yards Bar, she asked: "By the way, do you dance?""Gorgeous, that's one thing I did pick up in Texas. I hope you brought some heat, because I can move you around that floor like nobody's business."

———————— • ◆ • ————————

Dusk arrives early in January, Savannah observed as she was cleaning stalls about 5:00 that evening. Cade had work to do on his own stock, but he was also so helpful to her and Savannah loved it. He even helped exercise the heifers telling Eddie to grab three of Savannah's calves as they both lumbered away with pockets filled with can beer to help the girls stretch their legs. Savannah was sipping an absolutely slushy Crown and 7 when she looked up to see a man approaching at a rapid clip. The guy was moving at a quick enough pace that even above the settling noise of evening she could hear his cowboy boots tapping along purposely against the bricks. He wore a black cowboy hat and though the deep laugh lines around his eyes said he wasn't young, he wore a boyish and friendly look. In his gloved hand he carried a red plastic cup, presumably full of some kind of whiskey drink. She'd never seen him before, but for some reason she knew they were destined to meet. She tried to go back to work, but the sense of fate was so strong she simply paused, leaned against the pitchfork, and took a sip.

"Clint Cascade, and, you are Cade's Savannah Morgan," began the tall, friendly stranger without preamble as he ungloved his hand and extended it forcibly toward Savannah. "The pleasure is mine, though it would have been more so if I'd met you before Cade did," he said, revealing large brown eyes under the George Strait 20 X. Savannah instantly liked Clint Cascade; he acted as if they'd known each other for years. Upon closer inspection she noticed that he was older than her, probably a good 12 or 15 years at least, but he had a youthful air and style of dress that made him seem young even though he was surely over forty.

"Since you already know me, yes, I'll confirm, I'm Savannah Morgan. But, I'm not *Cade's* Savannah Morgan, despite what you've heard."

He looked genuinely concerned for a moment, then seeing that she was equal to his efforts at both wit and flirting he said enthusiastically: "Oh! Then there's still time to steal you away? I've stopped over up at Harbinger's before, but never left there madly in love. Perhaps it's worth revisiting the place!"

Savannah blushed at his remarks about Cade being in love with her. "Is that what he said to you?"

"The man's done and gone over you, which, like I said, is really too bad since I probably could have made you so happy, had I the chance," he said, clearly amused with himself. "Do you like yachts?"

"Do you like your ass whipped, Clancy?" came Cade's hearty voice from around the corner. He greeted Clint, now called Clancy, with total familiarity, but not as if he hadn't seen him in a while, in fact, Savannah noticed they didn't even shake hands, something she thought odd for two guys.

"*Clancy*?" The relationship between the two must be long term, she mused.

Cade chuckled and reached into his pocket for another icy Coors Light as he clamped the other man's shoulder affectionately. Clint winced just a tiny bit and Savannah noticed that although he had seemed tall enough alone, standing next to Cade he was made small in comparison.

"Savannah, this is Clancy Clinton Cascade the Third, rich investment banker from Maryland with no cattle sense whatsoever. Still, to his credit, he's my oldest friend and just so you don't go thinking he's hot, he's also an old man, way too old for a young lady like you," Cade said pulling Savannah to him possessively while he jeered at Clint. "I haven't even seen him in the yards yet, but leave it to him to appear out of thin air the moment I'm gone. Old Clance' can always find the pretty girls."

Cade's best friend is an East Coast investment banker?

"Hey, you're the one that told me to come see the love of your life. I'm just following direction," Clint shot back, looking at Savannah when he said it. "By the way, no one else but Cade and my mother call me Clancy. I hate it."

"That's why I do it, of course, and given that *it is* your name," stated Cade as he then stroked Savannah's head and pulled her to him just a bit tighter. "She's as perfect as I said, isn't she?" he said, clearly proud.

"If you say so, Man. She is beautiful. But, it's your fairy tale. I've never had the earth move for me, so it's whatever works for you. Got any more

Crown?" Clint remarked with a flip of his wrist and a gesture toward his plastic cup.

Savannah didn't appreciate being evaluated like a high-dollar heifer. "Hey! I'm here! You can talk to me!"

Who are these two guys, Simon and Simon?

Cade was all man while Clint was finer made and polished. That he was from the East Coast-she noticed the accent now-and was wealthy seemed completely contrary to what she thought she knew about Cade. It was evident the two were old friends. Different as they were in their look, voices, and mannerisms, they apparently got along well. As Cade reached in the showbox to retrieve the Crown, Clint stared at Savannah and smiled without ever moving his sharp brown eyes from her own. She was going to have to learn a lot more about Clint Cascade.

———————— • ◆ • ————————

By the time Cade and Savannah made their way up the stairs, it was late and the Yards Bar was hopping. The dank scent of spilled keg beer and the fog of cigarette smoke was nearly all that the senses could handle fresh in from the crisp Denver evening. A pleasant environment it was not, but it *was* the see-and-be-seen place on any night during the stock show. Ramshackle and just old, the bar, in the upstairs of the 1903 Stockyards Building, had absolutely nothing going for it in terms of looks. It was the crowd that made the place. The bar supposedly served food, though past about 6:00 nobody bothered trying to order much since service that didn't involve alcohol was slow and unlikely. Cowboys that had come in around 2:00 to conduct business and hadn't left occupied the few tables that lined the walls. The band had kicked up and the music was blaring. There wasn't really any way to hear each other talk, so Cade made good on his promise to dance as he led Savannah to the floor.

Two stepping with Cade was a blast. He was everything that any part-time buckle-rubber like Savannah could want in a dance partner. Cade's lead was immediate, his timing superb. He could dance to them all; the band covered George Strait, Brooks and Dunn, and Clay Walker, while Cade moved smoothly, sometimes pulling her in really close and kissing her neck, sometimes looping her arms around his head and back in a quick 'pretzel' move all while keeping the tempo right. She'd never had a dance partner so fun, or so sexy.

When the band finally took a break Savannah ran to the restroom; her face felt flushed and she had a beads of sweat on the bridge of her nose. She wanted to freshen up in case they kicked up the lights. The side door of the bar gave on to a narrow, window-lined breezeway that connected the second story bar to the Exchange Building. As usual, it was clogged with people either trying to get into the bar or waiting in line for the toilet.

"Savannah! Get over here!" cried a distinctively Oklahoman female voice. Macy's spot in line was mercifully close to the restroom door. Savannah quickly moved up amid nasty scowls from other women waiting. "She's really got to go, ok?" Macy remarked with a haughty look to the woman behind her. She opted to turn away rather than tangle with Macy.

"Wow! You and Cade Champion! He is sooo hot, Savannah!" Macy exclaimed as the girls embraced.

"You *heard* it already?" Savannah tried to smooth her hair and dab her face-the bright hallway lights were glaringly amplifying her red cheeks, she was certain.

"Honey, *everybody* knows. A guy like Cade is quite a piece of a-" Macy began, then cutting herself off, she peered at Savannah, perplexed. "It's 20 degrees outside and you're *sweating*?"

Savannah couldn't help but giggle. Macy noticed everything. "Well, Cade and I've been dancing-"

"For how long? My God, your hair is damp at the temples! Don't worry I've got a mini-sized can of this new stuff they're making called dry shampoo. It's in here someplace!" Macy began fumbling around inside an oversized cowhide and copper-studded purse.

Savannah just couldn't stop giggling. She thrust her hip out so Macy could balance the overflowing bag on her thigh. "You're right- its not just the dancing that's gotten me warm-I have a lot to tell you! This week I've been acting about like a heifer in heat!"

"I thought maybe my dancing was so bad you just up and left!" Cade remarked as Savannah sauntered back into the crowded bar, Macy in tow.

"Hey, there, Macy. How you and Stetson been?" Cade asked, smiling, while he reached for Savannah and pulled her in close.

"We're real good, Cade. He'll be in here any minute, he's out there on the damn phone." Macy playfully jabbed Cade in the ribs. "You and my sweet little friend, Savannah, huh? I never would have made the connection-but it looks like its working!"

"And I should have figured you two would be about the right age to be buddies. I'm hoping I can haul this one off the market the same way Stetson roped you!"

Savannah shot a fast and hard glance at Macy.

Crap! Her mind screamed, she had not told Macy that Cade wasn't fully versed on her martial status.

Macy, please get this look, please....

Macy, bless her soul, glanced back, confused, but sensed something was up.

"Oh Cade, I'm guessing you'll get that done as persuasive as you are, but you better earn it. Savannah is the best woman I know!"

"You got that right," he said, kissing Savannah's cheek.

"Hey, I'll catch you tomorrow, Girl," Macy announced. "I see some customers I better run and connect with. Meet you at the stalls about 11:00?"

———————— •◆• ————————

They were dancing again and this time Cade was driving her wild. Going from two-step to swing was exhilarating with Cade as her partner. He moved fast, turning her in and out of twirls and round-the-backs and whenever he had the chance to pull her close he'd push his pelvis into her or slide one hand way low on her hips. He breathed into her neck and even bit lightly at her ear. By the time the band had finished a particularly great rendition of '*The South's Gonna Do it Again*', Savannah was flushed from the closed heat of the crowd, from exhaustion, and from pure desire.

As Cade lifted her from a dip that had her long hair sweeping the dusty floor, Savannah kissed him.

"I need some fresh air and you-now!" she whispered hungrily.

Cade's brow raised in mock surprise and then his wide smile split into a broad grin that more closely resembled a leer. "Let's go!"

Outside, Savannah fell against Cade as the rush of frigid air stung her lungs. Cade pushed her up against the stone-cold brick wall of the alley behind the bar and kissed her until her lips ached with the impact. His hands roved while she leaned back and let him move his lips to her arched neck. "Let's go to the room."

Cade took her hand and led her into the cold night. Savannah gazed upward as she extended her neck back, stretching it and breathing in the refreshing cold air. Suddenly, her eyes raised just in time to meet a caustic glare. Eddie was standing above them on the balcony, puffing clumsily on a cigarette. He'd seen it all. Without bothering to chance his expression for Savannah's benefit, he tossed his cigarette down and stalked back toward the building.

———————— •◆• ————————

Eddie knew he was the only one blind enough not to believe that Cade and Savannah were fooling around. They'd been flirting for days and he was helping her with her stock like he owned them himself. Cade had taken up residence in Savannah's life and Eddie just hadn't wanted to see it. He shuffled toward the heavy door, causing the guy apparently leaning against the other side to fall right into him, practically knocking both of them down.

"Watch out asshole, that's a door you're holdin' up, not a wall," Eddie snapped. The guy who was busy picking himself up off his knees, straightened up, instantly ready for a fight.

"Who you callin' asshole, mutha-" the door-leaner cursed, but then his eyes brightened with recognition. "Eddie!" What's up man! Sorry about that!" laughed an obviously drunk Chet as he extended a hand. "Hey, how long you guys been here? We just got in tonight."

"Oh yeah," Eddie said off-handedly as he reached into his pocket for another cigarette. Normally, he detested the very thought of smoking but for some reason he'd picked up the habit.

"Yeah," Chet continued, flush-faced and oblivious to Eddie's terrible mood. "Just rolled in-been doing a little pre-partying in the pick-up since about Grand Island," the Nebraskan conceded, though it was obvious. "Where's my girl, Savannah?"

Eddie's laugh was not one of amusement. He scowled at Chet. The man was an idiot. So was he.

"Savannah's screwing some horse's ass named Champion out of Texas. She's so gone for him it about made me sick when I saw 'em makin' out just now. You're one dumb son-of-a-bitch if you think she'll look at you twice this week," Eddie remarked, saying everything to the crestfallen Chet that he knew was just saying out loud to himself.

———— •◆• ————

It was 10:00 before Savannah could get a grip on herself and actually focus on the work at hand. Things with Cade had escalated when they left the Yards Bar. For the first time since they'd met, there had been no talking in the truck and Cade had not left to go back to his hotel, either. Savannah's mind was barely able to stay in the present.

She was so dazed and unfocused that the most docile heifer had kicked her because Savannah had been so out to lunch that she'd startled the poor creature half to death. Still, she'd gone back into her Cade dreamland until Eddie's sharp yelp jarred her back to reality.

"What the hell is going on with you?" Eddie snapped as he nursed the spot on his thigh where the spooked heifer had made contact. "Just go back to bed with the asshole if you're not going to pay any better attention!" Eddie remarked caustically and was immediately sorry when he saw Savannah's expression of horror and hurt.

"Excuse me?" was all she could manage as she clicked off the blower and turned on her heel to reach for her not-so-warm coffee. Then, thinking better of it, she swung back around to face him. "I don't deserve that remark from you, Eddie. What I do with my personal life is none of your business!"

"Oh really? If it hadn't been for me, your precious 'personal life' at home would be a mess, but good ole Eddie just tolerates anything and goes with the flow-"

"Have I done something to piss you off? Is Cade's being around bothering you for some reason?" Savannah yelled loud enough that people nearby could hear the argument. Cade, who was just leading another heifer over from the wash rack stopped up short, an abrupt move that caused the heifer to skid a bit on the bricks.

154

"What's the problem with you, Quiggly?"

Savannah wore an expression that said she was about to cry.

"There's no f-n' problem, Champion." I'm going to take a leak." Eddie growled, hating himself for it, but his pride was hurting too bad to stop. He stamped one foot on the blower's power switch with enough force that besides shutting it off he broke the flimsy metal knob and sent it skidding across the pavement. Dropping the hose, he walked off.

"I've told you, Savvy, that you've got to ditch those damn Rockies!" reprimanded an exasperated Macy. "You'd really look so hot in Lucky's, but these will have to do. At least they are an update," she said, thrusting a pair of low-rise Cruel Girl Jeans at Savannah through the flimsy curtained-off area that was supposed to suffice as a fitting room.

The second story of 'the hill' barn was filled with vendors offering western wear, boots, rustic furniture, jewelry, and plenty more to please shoppers. Knowing school kids visiting the petting zoo and urban dwellers in pointy roach-killer boots would soon clog the aisles, the girls always went shopping early in the day.

Bella and Savannah were sandwiched in the makeshift changing area, a space the size of a phone booth that could barely hold another pair of jeans so overflowing as it already was with two girls, stacks of pants in an assortment of sizes, cute tops, and their own puff vests, jackets, and boots. "I'll try them on, I promise!" Savannah exclaimed amid laughs from Bella as she hopped on one foot trying to get her leg into the slim fitting jeans. "I really don't think it matters, anyway," she added bracing against Bella's shoulder for support. "I think Cade is pretty into me as it is and I probably should be sent to a convent for what I'm thinking about him!"

"Maybe so, but I told you at Louisville, you've got to dress like its the new millennium and the new millennium does NOT include jeans that make our back sides look like hams and press our lungs into our rib cages! Rockies are done! It's all low-rise, Girl!" Macy announced, then oblivious to the fact the Bella or Savannah might be in a state of undress, she yanked back the curtain. "Let's take a look!"

Savannah was just buttoning the fly of a pair of extremely snug Cruel Girl's that landed well below her belly button. Macy had also selected a tight, off-the-shoulder top in bright turquoise that Savannah had thrown on and had yet to situate just right. Macy reached out and began bodily adjusting her.

"God in Heaven!" she exclaimed, smacking Savannah's washboard-tight belly as she yanked the shirt into place, "If I had this figure there would be no stopping me! Girl, you are looking amazing!"

"As long as Cade thinks it looks good, then that's what I'm after," Savannah said, knowing how silly it sounded that she admitted wanting to look perfect just for a man.

"That bad is it?" Bella asked.

"Girls, I honestly don't know what's happened to me since I laid eyes on Cade Champion."

Over five hours had passed since Eddie had left. Savannah had ceased hoping that he would just return and all would blow over. It was the first moment that she'd been alone all day. She was just thinking about calling Eddie's cell and trying to smooth things over when Chet rounded the corner in a fury.

"Savannah!" I've been calling your cell since yesterday afternoon! How come you didn't call and let me know that you were stalled in?" Chet cried out, his arms open for a hug.

Even though he'd been stone-drunk the night before, Chet couldn't get the words Eddie had said about Savannah and some other guy out of his head. Though he'd wanted to run off and find her stalls as soon as they'd gotten up, he thought playing it cool and coming by after morning chores was a better idea. Besides, maybe Eddie was just in one of his characteristic bad moods. Though he'd told her after Christmas that he would give her space, he fervently wished that still meant an opportunity to hook up at Denver. "God you look gorgeous. I've missed you," Chet uttered as he wrapped her into a hug.

To Chet's disappointment, Savannah kept the hug light and quickly ducked her face as Chet leaned in to give her a kiss. "Chet, uh, how have you been?" she began awkwardly as she stepped away and pretended to be busy picking hairs out of a scotch comb.

"How have I been?" Chet cried, incredulous at her cool attitude. "I've been dying to see you, that's how! What's going on-what's Eddie talking about?" Chet grabbed her jacket, trying to pull her close.

"Chet, let go!" Savannah snapped and pulled back. He looked hurt.

"Come here, sit down. We need to talk right now," she commanded clearing a space on the showbox. Chet complying readily, but was beginning to feel nausea mount in his stomach; it wasn't from last night's whiskey.

Savannah attempted to smooth her hair behind a bejeweled earlobe just as the wind whipped it immediately back into her face. Chet reached for the tendril, and Savannah rose quickly, shoving back his hand.

"Chet! You've got to stop it. I don't know what Eddie must have told you, but whatever you've been holding onto, I'm really sorry, but I care for someone else."

Chet looked stung. Fast tears flooded his eyes and as he jumped up to grab her, Savannah backed away. "Chet, I mean it! Don't make this any harder than it already is. I care for you, but not in the way you think. Please, try to understand."

Chet steeled himself against crushing emotions. "What's his name?"

"Cade Champion."

Chet sprung up. "Eddie was right! You can't be serious, Savannah! That guy makes Tripp Crothers look innocent! Hell, everybody knows that type! They run around all over the road! What is it with you and the male whores you pick out?" Chet exclaimed. He was loosing Savannah to one of the cow businesses' biggest playboys. "Chet, he's not like Tripp," Savannah said, instantly tired. "He's been around, but I know he is not that type of guy. Cade warned me people would say that."

"He warned you because he knows that somebody will try to save you-"

"*Save me?*" This was just too much.

"Chet, you've been a friend, but I don't need saving-and I have never promised you anything!"

"Friend," Chet said flatly, looking a Savannah with the saddest eyes she'd ever seen. "That's not the way I saw it."

~ THIRTEEN ~

Yards Bar, Take II

Despite the day Savannah had endured between Eddie walking off and the heartbreaking exchange with Chet, she was drinking rather light for a Saturday in the Yards Bar. Macy and Bella were offering sympathetic ears while she related the Chet disaster and Cade was huddled at a table nearby with Stetson and Clint. The fun of the crowded, musky bar had worn off and all Savannah really wanted to do was go with Cade to the hotel.

It had been chore time before Eddie returned, so Savannah started feeding without him. Fortunately Cade had been there to help or she would have had to exercise the seven head alone. Eddie was sullen and didn't apologize for his attitude or for being gone all day, but Savannah accepted his help and just gave him space. Macy and Bella had pointed out that it was obvious that he was jealous as hell of Cade, but if that were true, Savannah felt like he was simply going to have to get over it. For that matter, so was Chet. Nothing in her nearly 25 years had prepared her for the axis-shift of meeting Cade and falling for him. Watching him talking to the other guys and thinking about touching him was just about as sexy as if she was sitting on his lap kissing him. Anyone who didn't like it or understand what she was feeling could just be damned.

Besides her multiple man troubles, with the sale being the next day, she was preoccupied with money concerns. Her funds were basically depleted and getting home on fumes was just about what she was looking at by the time she left Denver. Selling through the national sale wouldn't mean a check for a good 30 or 40 days, but it would be soon enough to hold off the feed elevator and Eddie's owed expenses, plus at least it would be a check. Problem was, how much? She needed the two pens to average $3,500 each just to cover what she owed and the bills she'd left at home. That, of course, would only solve the immediate problem and would leave nothing for the rest of the winter unless she simply went to shipping cows at the sale barn or mortgaging the farm. Savannah didn't want to part with any of the cows she had, the group was all pretty good and selling cows over the market in the winter wasn't usually good money. Doing a second mortgage was one idea, but that would mean that she'd failed at her job of managing the place. Harlan had not needed a second mortgage and it depressed her that she wasn't up to managing the finances. The fact remained that she had a stack of overdue bills, no 'job', and no experience in being the fulltime farm manager.

She hadn't admitted to Cade how much of a financial jam she was in, though he knew that she really wanted the sale to go well. So far Cade was so interested in her and talked all the time about how impressed he was that she could manage a cattle farm herself. She was genuinely afraid of jeopardizing the way that he looked at her. Telling him about Troy Howell would be bad enough.

"*Hello?* Anybody home?" Demanded Macy as she shook Savannah's arm; her friend had left the conversation for a full two minutes and was staring longingly in Cade's direction.

"You ever see a case this bad before?" she asked Bella with a grin.

"I've never had a sickness like she's got right now, that's for sure," Bella signaled the waitress to bring another round.

Savannah turned and faced her friends. "I have to say something. I think I'm falling in love with Cade Champion."

"Ya think?" Macy laughed.

───────── ◆ ─────────

"You two are too much!" Clint remarked as he tossed back the last of his whiskey. Another round was already awaiting the trio purchased courtesy of some guy hoping to win favor with Stetson. Cade had just winked at Savannah, *again*, a move that created an eruption of giggles from the girls. When Savannah blew him a kiss, Clint thought Cade acted like an idiot teenager that had just copped his first feel. Never had he seen his old friend so bewitched. Clint, a single man not inclined to believe in love, found their actions pathetic. "I swear if you make one more candy-assed, sappy look at that girl, I am leaving this bar and heading straight for the strip club!"

Stetson burst into laughter. "Ah, com' on, Cascade. Ain't you ever seen a guy in love before? Hell, it's kind of funny watching him act like a dumb ass."

"It would be funny if it just wasn't so embarrassing to the whole entire male gender. Cade, you're going to give that girl the wrong idea, besides. She's gonna think you are a good, wholesome catch or something," Clint added, stirring his whiskey in agitation and tossing the straw on the filthy floor.

Cade beamed. "That's a good word for me - wholesome! Yes, Savannah and I are like a wholesome, happy couple. I am gonna marry that girl, you just watch." Cade said confidently, raising his glass and toasting the thought.

Both guys simultaneously guffawed at the prospect of Cade Champion off the market.

"The thought of her making an honest man out of you is hilarious, Champion. But, she's not as innocent as you think! Last I heard she still had man problems to clean up back at home. 'Course that could be settled by now, I don't know. Macy hasn't-"

Just as Cade turned to question Stetson's comments, he was interrupted by a heavy shove to his shoulder blades. Completely caught off guard, the move pushed Cade forward and he hit the table edge hard with both palms, one nearly upsetting it and the other cracking the whiskey glass in his right hand.

"I'm callin' you out, Champion! Stand up and fight me like a man!" yelled Chet as he wobbled slightly from the effort of his strike.

"What in the f-" Cade exclaimed, turning to meet to perpetrator as he began picking glass chunks from his bloody palm. Seeing the young man was obviously drunk and acting the fool, Cade attempted to cool him off.

"Look, buddy, you're drunk, you got the wrong man."

"I got the right guy, asshole, but you ain't gonna get Savannah that easy," Chet cried out as he awkwardly landed a punch across Cade's upper lip.

"Chet! Get a hold of yourself! Stop It!" Savannah screamed, trying to make her way to the men. The scene was already alive with spectators and in the crowded bar attempting to quickly cover the distance between a few tables was almost impossible.

Clint and Stetson were struggling to pull Chet back, but whiskey and desperation make for a determined man. Chet fought loose just as his friends were near enough to reign him in. "Come on, fight me! Fight me!" Chet yelled in Cade's direction, throwing punches as he flailed against Stetson's grip.

Savannah finally broke through the crowd and reached out to Chet.

"Calm down, Chet!" she yelled above the assembled mass, but Chet was so lost in his own rage that he couldn't hear her. He kept jousting wildly until one of his random punches mistakenly landed across the point of Savannah's chin sending her sprawling backward into the table behind them. As she fell, chairs overturned, people scattered amid the spray of drinks, food, and glass shattering everywhere. Macy and Bella scrambled to pick her up before she landed on the floor.

The lion-like roar Cade emitted seemed to shake the rafters. He yanked Chet clean from Stetson's stunned grasp and briefly held him upright before landing a punch square to his face. Chet hung limp, his head flopping back and forth like a boomerang. "Easy buddy! Lay off, Man!" Hollered Marty as he attempted to intervene. *Everybody* knew of Cade Champion; the thought of him kicking Chet's stupid ass made Marty want to puke. "I'm so sorry he accidently hit her! He didn't mean it!" Marty cried out again.

Yet Cade had already pulled Chet up and swiftly clobbered him with yet another blow, this time sending him back across a chair where he hung like a dripping wet rag.

"It was an accident, Cade!" Clint called out. In 30 years of knowing him, he'd never seen Cade fight. They'd been in scrapes, mostly involving smart remarks or girls they should have left alone, but Cade had always looked the intimidating part with his size and heft while Clint talked their way out of it. "Hold on, Cade!" Clint attempted again. "He didn't mean it-he's just a drunk!" Clint reached out to Cade as he exchanged worried glances with Stetson. They had to stop him. He was literally pulverizing the skinny kid.

"You've got to get up, Savannah," Macy rasped sternly in the ear of her dazed friend. "Cade's not going to hear anyone but you and he's about to kill poor, stupid, Chet."

Knowing the truth of it, Savannah righted herself, pausing just half a beat to breathe and get her footing before advancing toward Cade.

"Cade, it's okay! He nearly missed me. I'm fine –it's okay!" Savannah stressed the last point again as she moved, cautiously at first, to Cade's side.

He saw her and abandoned his grip on Chet's shirt collar, a move that deposited the bludgeoned boy in a sagging heap. Marty hustled to prop him up while Clint grabbed napkins to stop the bloody sieve that was Chet's nose.

"Are you alright? What the hell is going on with this dude?" Cade reached for Savannah and pulled her close. "Are you sure you're okay?" he asked again, holding her cheek just a little harshly as he examined the spreading bruise along her jaw.

Suddenly, Clint was by Cade's side. "Man, listen to me, you've got to get the hell out of here. Somebody's called those rent-a-cop bouncers and they'll be hauling you in-"

"Take my truck-it's parked right out behind the bar," Stetson reasoned, pressing a set of keys into Cade's hand. "Get him the hell off these fairgrounds now!" he grabbed Savannah's arm to make the point. "We'll get this kid out the back door."

Two thick-necked guys in black t-shirts were already approaching through the thinning crowd, but Macy and Bella made a play for getting in their way. Though brief, the effort bought Savannah and Cade just enough time; they escaped through the breezeway and out the side of the Exchange Building.

Cade didn't speak in the truck, but he held so tightly to her left hand that it hurt as her rings pinched into the flesh of her fingers. Still, Savannah didn't dare pull her hand back. Had she thought better of it, she wouldn't have let him drive, but he was so intense and they had needed to get gone fast, so she didn't fight it.

At the hotel, he slammed the truck into park and grabbed her around the shoulders a little roughly as they headed inside. Cade was more aggressive than she'd ever seen him, kissing her passionately in the elevator even as she tried to start apologizing for Chet. Cade didn't listen.

They fell together in the room, Cade both pulling away at her clothes and his until he carried her naked to the bed. He kept mumbling about how he wanted her and didn't know what was going on and why some other guy wanted to fight him. Savannah tried to answer, but Cade clearly didn't want to hear it. The heat of their passion was so overwhelming Savannah couldn't think straight enough to form words anyway. Suddenly, Cade pulled back, now gentler, his eyes full of tears.

"I'm in love with you, Savannah." The way he gazed at her melted her insides.

"Do you love me back?"

"I'm madly in love with you, Cade," she whispered.

"Then show me," he breathed huskily.

———————— •◆• ————————

Later, Cade held Savannah as she tucked up against his waist, fitting perfectly. He wanted to ask about the guy back home situation, but the sound of her sniffles caused him to pause.

"What's going on, Savannah?" Cade asked, tucking his chin into her shoulder and then whispering in her ear. "Wasn't that good enough for you? We can try again if you need me to make some improvements." His good-natured humor had returned, though he was still unsure about what had happened back at the bar.

Savannah snugged up closer but as she turned to him, she broke into sobs.

"Tell me what's going on."

"I'm just a little preoccupied, I guess. I'll be honest, I really need these heifers to sell. It hasn't been easy since Dad died in October. Let's just say, I wasn't exactly ready to take over everything - its not like I haven't tried - but I-"

"How bad is it, Savannah?"

"It's relatively bad," she began.

It's just so humiliating!

She hated the thought of telling him that she really didn't know what she was doing or that she had no money lined up on the heifers.

"Talk to me, Savannah," Cade urged as he pushed them into a seated position. The bruise on her chin was already darkening and she had a knot where Chet had dumbly made contact. Cade touched it lightly. "Come on, I took a punch for you, Young Lady," he added, rubbing the swelling on his upper lip. "I can't help you if you don't tell me what you need. I told you, I love you."

Savannah put her head down again and through a flood of shameful tears, she told Cade everything. She shared all of her fears about money and about the fact that she knew it was a foolish to bring Tiara out and attempt to win Denver.

Later, the talk turned to them and how he might come back to her place after he got through the Ft. Worth show. He pondered how he could even move his cows there and consider finding another firm to work for that wasn't so far away. That they had a future together was not a question in Cade's mind.

By the time Savannah fell asleep, she had shared everything with Cade - everything except the fact that she was still legally married.

Watching her, Cade felt as close to Savannah as he ever had to any other human being. She needed him and she had confided in him, but he couldn't shake the nagging feeling about what Stetson had started to say.

Surely there isn't more she's leaving out, Cade wondered again, but he convinced himself that maybe the deal back at home was related to the farm or the bills. She was obviously a strong and determined woman.

Savannah slept on, her eyes now puffy, but her breathing steady and restful. Cade knew that he loved her and that making her happy was the most important thing he could accomplish in his life. It amazed him how much one woman could endure for the love of her farm and for the love of showing cattle. Savannah was the kind of woman he'd been searching for but never realized it until they met.

Cade hatched a few ideas about how to secure his place in her heart.

~ FOURTEEN ~

Cattle deals

"These heifer's of Savannah's shaped up pretty decent after I got them blocked out," Cade observed as he stepped out of the stall bed, unwrapped his second breakfast sandwich, and began devouring it. With no formal obligations at the show, Clint had decided to bring breakfast by for Savannah and Cade's crews. He figured it had been a long night after the fight. They looked worn out, but still happy, and Clint was glad of it. More than that he was glad his old friend hadn't been hauled to jail.

Savannah and Eddie were nearby blowing out the last heifer in the group. Soon they'd let the stock reset for a few hours before fitting them for the 4:00 pm sale.

"Yeah, they're really pretty decent, especially once you got to working on them."

"So, uh, does that mean you like them?"

"Sure, yeah, they're nice enough. A little line-bred and they could use some updated pedigrees but they'd be great base cows," Clint observed. "Why?"

Cade smirked and shoved the rest of the ham, egg, and cheese in his mouth as he slurped on a gigantic coffee.

"Oh, no, you're not expecting me to –"

Cade put his hands up as if in desperation. "You know I'd buy them for her if I could, but until after weaning I haven't got a dime not tied up in those receipt cows I own down at the Bow String."

"Has she got *any* money on them?" Clint queried.

"I don't think so. You know she'll get a handful of sympathy bids because some people knew her Dad. I mean, she said Harlan and the sale manager go way back, but you know how much that accounts for," Cade remarked as he and Clint exchanged eye-rolls. It was well known that sales managers expected consigners to bring their own live money to the auction. "Hey, I get it. These pedigrees *are* dated and the heifers needed somebody besides that lazy Quiggly feeding and clippin' on 'em the last two months. But, you know-"

Clint glanced toward Savannah. She was clad in a bright yellow Columbia jacket, her blonde hair shimmering as it fluttered around her shoulders. Even wearing black snow pants to ward off the frigid morning, her trim figure was evident. She was working hair on the best heifer, alternating between brushing intently and then stepping back to view her work. The serious expression on her face didn't dampen her youthful beauty; Clint could see why Cade was enamored. Hell, he was half enamored with her, too.

Who wouldn't be? Clint thought to himself.

She was barely 25, blonde, beautiful, fresh-faced, witty, and yet more innocent than any woman he'd met in years. She could get any man in the cow business to fall in love with her and she didn't even know it.

Bemused – at himself and at Cade - he said: "What's it like to be so whipped?"

"You wish you knew." Cade said knowingly as he clamped his old friend on the shoulder.

Clint flinched slightly. He sure did.

———————— •◆• ————————

By 3:00 that afternoon, the six heifers were all on display outside of the sale facility. Savannah and Eddie had gotten them up there and the crowd was beginning to swell the aisles with people looking at all the pen cattle. Savannah's insides were swimming. The calves looked so nice - Cade had seen to that - but she really didn't have anything more than 'interest' in a couple of them. Her sale order didn't make it look very promising either; being in the bottom third of the sale was never a good thing. She was beginning to fret.

Cade had gone back to check on his crew but assured Savannah he'd meet her back at the stalls and stick with her during the sale. She was anxious to get over to the sale area; leaving Eddie to do any kind of promoting was a terrible idea. If only she could just call Cade and tell him she was heading back.

He has got to get a cell phone!

But, suddenly, he appeared and always seemingly carefree, he grabbed an icy beer out of the cooler before approaching her.

Savannah didn't mean to be peevish, but she was nervous and didn't want to be kept waiting. "I wish you had a cell phone, Cade!"

"Why would I need one? Then people would just bother me!" His arms circled her waist in a powerful hug. "Of course, I'd like you to know where I am at all times, so maybe I'll get one after Ft. Worth."

"I'd like that if I could keep better tabs on you," she added, softening. Cade had a way of making her feel like all was going to be okay. She pulled away and began gathering a handful of supplies to take back to the sale ring.

"What's this I hear about 'a guy back home' and the poor kid who split my lip?" Savannah stiffened.

I have to face this! Her mind screamed.

She'd start with the easy topic.

"It's my fault about Chet. We met at Louisville –he really is a sweet guy-but, I let him get too close. I didn't mean for it to happen, but he pushed and I just didn't have the energy to do what I should have which was tell him I wasn't interested. He literally came by the house, *from Nebraska*, over Christmas. I told him not to, but he showed up anyway. Then my mother arrived and invited him to stay, which he did for a few days. We never slept together, Cade, but he just kept holding out hope even when I told him it wasn't going to work."

Cade smiled, filled with relief. If that was all, then he probably had nothing to worry about. She didn't seem too interested in the Nebraskan. He even felt a bit bad about how harshly he'd hit him. "So that must be what Stetson mentioned about 'a guy back at home, then?"

Savannah shifted uncomfortably and looked away. Now was her chance, Cade was asking her to be honest.

I have to tell him!

Savannah took a deep breath, thinking she would quickly relate the story of Troy and just get it out in the open. "Well, Cade, actually - "

"You're not much of a saleswoman being back at the stalls while your stock are on display!" Announced Clint as he cantered up at his typical brisk pace. He eyed Savannah closely, noting that the bruise on her chin had darkened over the course of the day. A little dried blood crusted over Cade's lip. "You two look like hell, but I've got to talk with you anyway. So, Savannah, I wondered if you might be willing to do something?"

"Uh, sure Clint. What?" Savannah was knocked off guard again, both relieved and frustrated about the interruption.

"Well, I'm looking to make an investment. But, you see, as The Great Cade Champion knows, I don't have time or inclination to keep up much of a livestock facility back at my place. So, Savannah, beautiful, bewitching love of Cade's life-would you consider partnering with me on your six heifers?"

Savannah was stunned.

Would she! Of course!

"Wow! I mean, really, Clint?" she didn't care that she sounded every bit the rookie.

"Well, now, don't get so excited-there is always a catch in every deal that I make. You haven't heard my terms!"

"Whatever they are-yes!" Savannah was like an enthusiastic child.

"Well, in that case, I have some very, very interesting ideas-"

"Put a cork in it Clance!" Cade countered, with humor that bordered on slight irritation. He pulled his sunglasses down just a tad and raised one of his dark, heavy brows as if in challenge.

Clint ignored him and laughed. "Well, really, they're pretty simple. You keep them, house them, feed them, etc. and we'll split the breeding costs and split the proceeds, but you get an extra 10 percent for the work."

"I can't believe you're doing this, Clint, that's amazing!" Savannah said, pulling free from Cade's arm and reaching to give Clint a warm hug.

Clint accepted it with a wry smile; she really was too sweet and beautiful to be near for long. No wonder Cade was such a mess. He pushed her back gently, reclaiming his playful, jesting style. "Of course - I mean, if they start to bring big money, like over ten grand a round or something, well, I'd have to be out, you understand, I hope."

Savannah's lashes fluttered at the notion of $10,000 a head for the heifers.

That would be impossible!

"Why yes," Clint continued. "I couldn't make a commitment that high-after all- I wouldn't be able to afford my summer golf trip to Scotland!"

Cade looked mildly annoyed as Savannah hugged Clint again.

The mission was accomplished even if he did need to keep one eye open around his oldest friend.

———————— •◆• ————————

"Oh, Eddie! Isn't it amazing! We're going to be able to keep going when we get home. I've been so worried, but it's going to be okay! The heifers averaged $7,500! I cannot believe it!" Savannah was rattling on, clearly elated. They were tying in the last of the heifers following the sale.

True to his word, Clint Cascade had bought both pens. The first he'd gotten reasonably enough at $5,500 a round, but the second pen had cost him $8,750 apiece. Apparently, Cade had confided to Savannah as they stood ringside afterward, when cowboys note that a guy like Clint is bidding they take notice by raising their hands, too. The last thing any guy who thinks he's a somebody (and there were plenty of them in the show cattle business!) wants is to be left out on something hot!

Eddie was glad for Savannah – until he realized the damn stock were returning to Indiana; now he would have to work on them back at home, too.

Pain in my ass! Eddie was thinking as he grabbed a fork and began half-heartedly working a little fresh bedding into the stalls.

Savannah continued, oblivious to Eddie's irritation. "Cade, and especially Clint, really made this happen. I'm so, well, *wow*, I guess, I'm just so happy, Eddie!" she reached over and started to put her arm around his slumped shoulders. Eddie had been barely listening to her and he was surprised when she reached over to hug him. She smiled that little sexy smile that made Eddie's natural melancholy subside for a moment.

"I know you've been a tad grouchy about Cade being around, Eddie, but you're going to have to get used to it," Savannah gushed, then wistfully she added. "He's coming to Indiana, Eddie. Cade and I have been talking, we're in love and he is planning to move to Indiana to be near me."

Bile rose in Eddie's throat like a volcano.

Cade Champion moving to Indiana?

My life could not get any worse.

And then, as if by some sick black magic, Savannah's knight suddenly appeared. "Hey, Ed! Don't tie them in, Man! Pull those halters and let's just feed. Hell, it's time to celebrate!" exclaimed Cade Champion, who, lithe as a panther strode up, pulled Savannah from his arms, and whisked her away all while he bossed Eddie around like a common laborer.

Savannah's eyes shone like diamonds. Cade was her prince.

Eddie swallowed his puke.

"Stand right where you are, you, two!" Commanded Macy as she pulled a pink digital camera from her handbag. "I want to capture this adorable moment with Savannah and her high-sellers!"

"High-sellers, indeed!" Clint chimed in. "I just wrote a check for over $40,000! That second pen was just the high selling heifer pen in Denver!" Clint shook his head, but he was laughing.

"Aw, Clance, get up here and grab a photo with us-just think of all the publicity and lime light you'll get for buying the high sellers!" Cade countered, as Clint crowded into the photo and Macy began snapping shots. Cade was right, of course. Clint loved to be considered a wheel.

"It is time to celebrate. Let's go to dinner at the Broker."

"You buying?" Laughed Stetson as he reached for a beer and then tossed several more, one after another, toward the trio. Cade, like a juggler, didn't miss a beat, grabbing them in succession and passing one each to Savannah and Clint.

Clint, popping his top, reached an arm around Savannah's waist and pretended to pose like a Shepler's model. "Oh, hell yes I'm buying. Why stop now?"

"Then it is a celebration!" Cade cheered, and not to be out done by his friend, he pulled Savannah into a deep dip, kissing her all the way.

Macy snapped photos faster than a Hollywood paparazzi.

An hour later, the stock had been fed and watered and it was dark. The little group of revelers had been drinking hard. Drake Jones had even come by to congratulate Savannah, saying she was welcome in any of his sales anytime. The owner of a big commercial outfit from South Dakota was talking to Clint about getting in on half of the second pen; Clint was making a show of how he couldn't possibly let the group go at this point, but that he'd keep the man in mind for a flush. Disappointed and slightly irked, the South Dakotan ambled away. Cade, totally amused, poured Clint another whiskey and slapped the thin man on the back amid guffaws from Stetson.

Eddie had been cleaning up and drinking plenty of whiskey, too. He had turned surly. When Clint hollered at him to leave for dinner, Eddie declined saying he would stay behind to lock up. Savannah smiled at him, thanked him, and left with the group.

After waiting five minutes to make sure no one doubled back, Eddie opened the showbox. He'd seen Macy carelessly toss the digital camera in a drawer. Pulling it out, he removed the little memory chip card and then replaced the camera just as he'd found it.

He had to make a stop at the hotel's business center.

———————— •◆• ————————

I just can't get this timing correct!

Savannah had been agonizing over the issue of Troy and it was only getting worse the closer they were to leaving Denver. Now, with what he and Clint had done for her the last thing she could do was disappoint Cade. Plus, show day was tomorrow and they'd be leaving the following morning. She finally decided telling Cade about Troy would have to wait until his first visit to Indiana. She just prayed that he'd understand and that maybe she'd even have the divorce final by then.

Now, as she and Macy were devouring the signature shrimp cocktail and the bottle of Vueve Cliquot that Clint had ordered, Savannah couldn't help but notice how sexy the men looked talking with each other.

I must not have had hormones before I met Cade.

It was like even the smallest things about him drove her absolutely *wild*. Before Cade, boys were cute or boys were not. Or, boys were fun or boys were dull. Savannah really wasn't that much more interested in them, at least not long term. It occurred to her that was why she'd tolerated living with Troy – it just hadn't mattered. Being married, sad to say, just hadn't mattered, either. But, now, with Cade, *everything* mattered.

All the guys she'd known before had been just that: just boys.

Until Cade.

--------------------- • ◆ • ---------------------

"You got any stroke with that Prioleaux judging the female show tomorrow?" Cade asked, knowing the answer. Winston Prioleaux was from South Carolina and ran about the only decent major Angus operation in the South East. Given that Rawlings Ranch dealt in Angus, Cade knew Stetson would have something to say.

"Sure, why?"

"Does she have any shot in hell tomorrow?"

He, Clint, and Stetson flipped through the next morning's show program. They'd just come across the January division. Savannah and Tiara had not broken into an easy class; the heifer that had won Louisville was slated to be in it as was the high-dollar female that had just won Reno.

"I'd say it'll be tough, well, more than tough, unlikely, really," said Clint as he swirled his glass of cabernet.

"Yeah, I know it. The heifer really is looking good, considering she's been worked on by Quiggly, but man, if I'd had her at my place for the last two months, we could have got her feet trimmed and fed her different and I woulda-"

"Cade, you act like Savannah is incompetent, and I don't think you actually believe that," Stetson interrupted. He'd never seen Cade worried before show day.

"Well, I just don't want her to get disappointed, ya know?" Cade said, sipping his red and glancing over at the girls. "Maybe I otta just tell her to scratch."

"Why would you do that? Maybe she'll find herself in the Championship Drive." Clint said, then added, "But maybe not. This is Denver and not some Podunk state fair. Has that Tiara female actually won anything?"

"She won a division in Kansas City, but got left stand."

"What'da ya think, Stetson? What's old Pru gonna do?"

Stetson paused, turning to watch Macy and Savannah giggling yet again about something only girls would find funny. He wished he could feel about Macy again the way Cade felt about Savannah. They'd been the foregone conclusion of a power couple marriage-partnership for so long that he'd forgotten what being in love felt like.

"You know, you two guys just might be the biggest conservatives I've ever met. Why not roll the damn dice, let her show, and see what happens?" Stetson queried, almost in irritation, as he regarded his two friends. The two were thumbing through the show program as though reading it foretold that the show's outcome was already written in stone. He'd known Clint and Cade since their first junior nationals and they'd been around the show cattle industry as long as anybody he knew. They knew the ups and downs of this deal; if you showed one you had two chances – you either won or you got beat. Simple as that. Anyone who had shown as much as them knew the highs of the big win and the metallic taste of disappointment when you were sure you had a win in the bag – and it turned out you didn't. It was like they'd forgotten what it was like just to *hope* that you might win when you actually had a nice one on the trailer. Stetson thought

Savannah's innocence was good for Cade. He thought about saying it, but didn't.

"You can't predict an old-time breeder like Prioleaux. He probably doesn't even read the damn magazines but, he probably did know of Harlan. So, who the hell knows? Cade, he might actually just like the damn heifer and use her!"

Cade and Clint looked up, surprised. Stetson didn't give many speeches when he wasn't on the mic at ringside.

Stetson just stared at Cade. "What's with you going down without a fight, Champion?"

IN THE HUNT

Grand Champion Drive

Denver, 2000

She pulled her back into alignment with the group, edging just a shade in front of the Fall Division Champion behind her, pausing only to wipe the spit off Tiara's muzzle with her shirt cuff. The heifer blustered a tad in protest at the affront, but as if knowing it was necessary, immediately raised her head up and out . Savannah tapped Tiara's off-show-side front hoof to tuck it closer to the other and straightening her arm to its full extended length, stepped back to view what she knew would be her final pose. Tiara looked perfect.

They'd made three laps around the ring, though the coliseum floor was unforgiving, unlike the carpet of green shavings that blanketed Louisville's famous Freedom Hall. Like everything in Denver, you worked harder for it. The ring was smaller, the dusty base hard and pocked by the day's end with thousands of hoof marks. Navigating it took patience and possibly maneuvering to get a good spot once you were stopped. You didn't want your heifer's front end running down hill by parking her in a rutted up spot. Looking now, Savannah was satisfied with her location and the angle. Tiara stood motionless, breathing without effort. Savannah attempted to check her breath, it was coming in gasps, she thought of scanning the ring for Cade, but resisted the urge.

She needed to focus.

The judge had made his final speech while Savannah repositioned. Now, the ring and crowd were silent. Time had slowed. Savannah's breath was unnatural, she wheezed and sensed that her legs were braced. Prioleaux briskly walked the length of his line up, not eyeing any single heifer, giving nothing away about his impending choice. Then, he abruptly turned back again. Savannah watched him, stared at him, focused on his expression as he moved intently past first the calf champion, then the intermediate, then the summer division, then the spring borns, and he edged closer to her. Savannah felt her stomach flip, she felt the tinge of small smile form at her lips, lips that were so dry with cotton mouth so bad she could barely swallow. She hoped he'd pause, he was nearing her. He'd passed five other division winners.

He couldn't possibly want the senior yearling...

Why isn't he extending his hand?

Right as he could have –should have- paused, he passed her. Savannah felt disbelief crowd her heart, but on instinct her eyes followed him as he also passed by the front of the senior yearling , the last heifer in the Grand Drive.

Suddenly, the judge stopped and flamboyantly doubled back, breaking into a broad grin and gesturing boldly as he pointed right at her. He hustled to slap Tiara on the rump.

"You young lady, have a nice one!" Prioleaux announced as he extended his hand and removed his hat.

For her.

For Tiara.

The sound of Savannah's own shriek of joy filled the coliseum to the rafters.

A WIN!

A *DENVER* WIN!

~ FIFTEEN ~

Broken Hearts

Savannah was floating on air as she led Tiara from the ring with one hand, her showstick and the purple and gold Grand Champion banner swaying jauntily in her left. Eddie was there immediately with a half-hearted smile and hug while he helped lead Tiara to the backdrop. As the photographers started to position them for the winning photo, Savannah was distracted; she was hungry to see Cade, for him to hold and kiss her, for him to be proud of her at this moment.

Where is he?

She scanned the crowd wildly. He'd been at ringside just before she stepped in for the Grand Drive, but now he'd vanished. If he'd gone off to the restroom or to talk with some other friend, he'd picked a poor time, Savannah mused with irritation. It took nearly 15 minutes to pose the heifer correctly between Tiara's impatience (the big bred had been standing for nearly three hours) and the time it took to get the judge there and then to add in the queens and sponsors. Still, all the while, no Cade. Clint was at the backdrop to congratulate but said he had no idea where Cade was.

Savannah accepted congratulations and hugs from friends and even people she didn't know. She could barely contain her tears of joy.

I've just won Denver! I've just won Denver! Her mind was reeling with delight.

But cold, nauseating fear was starting to seep into the warmth of Savannah's happiness.

Where is Cade?

"Macy, have you seen him?" she asked, starting to panic, as Macy hugged her tightly.

"Huh! Where the hell is he, anyway?" Macy's brow furrowed only momentarily before she perked back to her usual delighted state. "Well, I'm sure he's headed back to the Yards to prepare something great for you-a celebratory surprise maybe! We're going to have a hell of a party tonight! Hey! Don't fret it, okay?"

Savannah smiled wanly. She hoped so. "Ask Stetson if he's seen him, will you? I can't believe he missed seeing her win!" she complained, scratching Tiara's poll affectionately.

Macy was right; she had to be. In fact, it *was* true, Cade didn't think much of pomp and circumstance, so the backdrop hoopla probably didn't appeal to him. She wished he had considered what it would have meant to her to have him there - and she would have to talk with him about that later – but, yes, *surely* he was back at the stalls and had dispatched one of his crew boys to buy beer for a party.

It had been a good hour since she'd won and still no Cade. Savannah and Eddie were leading Tiara down through the yards back to tie out for the evening and she was nearly hysterical, now convinced that Cade had an emergency come up.

But what? Damn it! He needed a cell phone!

She was going to insist that he buy one immediately. He could have at least told her what was wrong or left word before he ran off without notice. Savannah was both angry and afraid. As she turned into the yards pen, her hopes were finally dashed. Instead of Cade smiling smugly and looking at her with that stunning mischievous grin, the only thing out of the ordinary was the brown manila envelope plastered on the door of her showbox with two pieces of gray tape.

"URGENT CORRESPONDENSE"
To Be Opened Immediately
To: Cade Champion
From: Troy Howell
RE: Savannah Morgan Howell

Savannah felt herself start to swoon. She tore at the tape, ripping the envelope as she fought to pull it open. The contents spilled to the ground as bile gurgled in her throat. Streaming out of the torn envelope was the black and white proof of her life story – all the parts of it that she had not told Cade: a copy of her marriage license, a wedding picture, and a crudely typed letter from Troy. The air went out of Savannah's lungs. A deafening noise like the sound of a train flooded her ears as she fell her knees to retrieve the letter.

Hello, Cade. You don't know me, but apparently you know my wife, Savannah Morgan Howell. Looks like you two have been having plenty of fun while she was away from home. Either keep your hands off, or if she's that important, you can have her, but I'll need a check. Divorce is expensive.

Tears came in sobs, breathing felt like trying to inhale clumps of dirt. Then she noticed handwriting on the back of the envelope.

Savannah,

A courier just handed me this. I don't even know what to say – I thought it was love, I never would have guessed you'd deceive me this way. I would have married you. I wanted to be with you. I would have never guessed you were still married to someone else. How could you not have told me?

– Cade

Moments later Savannah was racing through the yards. Blinded by tears, her hair partly matted to her face, she dodged the people and cattle crowding the brick alleys on the way to tie-outs. Slipping on the ice, she fell but paused only briefly to notice her ripped her jeans and bloodied kneecap, but it didn't matter. She burst into the pen where Cade's ranch had made stalls. Her lungs were swollen with cold air from gasping in the horror that Cade had found out this way.

She was too late. The Bow String Ranch signs had been hastily pulled down and the gates had been lifted, leaving strange squares of bark where stalls had just been. A deflated bag of shavings flapped in the cold wind around the empty pen.

Cade was gone.

PART IV

Savannah's Choices

~ SIXTEEN ~

Eddie's chance

Four weeks and no Cade.

Though she never said one word to him about it, Eddie knew Savannah had tried everything to reach Cade. It hadn't worked. Cade was as elusive as if he had never existed. Through the network that is the livestock showing industry, Savannah learned that he returned from Denver and abruptly quit the Bow String Ranch, a move that apparently startled his boss and didn't sit well with him, either. Sounded like Cade burned a bridge he shouldn't have, but he had a real 'go-to-hell' attitude, so somebody said, and apparently didn't care that he'd just pissed off a billionaire.

Clint Cascade stopped by unannounced about a week and a half after they got home on the premise that he came to see his new investment. Savannah had been so excited to see him and Eddie could tell she was grilling the man endlessly about Cade's whereabouts but if Clint knew anything, he didn't tell her. Eddie overhead him saying something about the fact that she should get real about silly things like love at first sight. Eddie thought he was just being an ass.

Savannah was so down after his lack of news that she went to the house without seeing him off, leaving Eddie to rely Clint's message that he would have semen shipped to breed the heifers and that he'd stop by again next time he was in town.

Eddie hoped he never came back.

Via Macy, Stetson had told Savannah that he hadn't even seen Cade in Fort Worth, a show he hadn't missed working in nearly 20 years. Cade had called Stetson briefly and told him only that he was planning on going 'up North' to free lance for a big ranch, but he didn't mention which one or when he planned to start. Stetson said Cade was so broken up over Savannah that he didn't expect to hear from him for a while and that she should just be patient. Savannah didn't really believe him.

One evening while Eddie did chores he watched as Savannah sat on the back porch, shivering in the late January dusk and crying while she talked with Macy on the phone. Cade may not have vanished, but he didn't want to be found by Savannah.

Eddie hated Cade Champion.

Eddie hated himself more.

Most of all, though, Eddie was sick of seeing Savannah so down and he knew it was his fault. He'd begun to admit to himself that Savannah had really loved Cade and he had stood in her way of happiness. To make matters worse, the bastard Troy Howell still wouldn't give up and agree to divorce. Jessica had tried to intervene telling Savannah that she would sell off a few acres of the farm and use the proceeds to pay Troy to leave. But Savannah had been insulted and vehemently refused. Eddie thought maybe she should do it and said so. That he said it infuriated her and he regretted it. She told Eddie it didn't matter if she was still married to Troy because no one else wanted her anyway.

Most of his life, Eddie knew that he lacked courage. He always tried to avoid problems, his own and other people's. Meddling was never something that interested him and he had always kept a low and status quo profile. He'd made a terrible mistake in getting involved with Savannah and Troy's mess. The big mistake he made was being jealous and being a jerk. He knew it. Now, he was terrified about admitting it to Savannah. He was drinking too much, sleeping too much, and he was in as big a funk as she was.

———— •◆• ————

As usual on Wednesday evenings, Eddie was drinking in the track bar. He was probably already four beers in and had just ordered another and some wings, when he saw Troy walk in. Eddie's first reaction was to leave. He hadn't talked to him since the day he'd had the hotel staff print the pictures of Savannah and Cade after the Denver sale, then faxed them to Troy and received Troy's fax back in return – a package of papers that he then put in the hotel envelope and crudely paid a punk to deliver. Cade had gotten the package at ringside while Savannah was walking Tiara in for the Grand Champion drive. The sight of Troy made Eddie ill, but before he could gather some cash and pay, something odd about Troy's behavior gave him pause. Obscured by the height of the booth and some of the bar's crowd, Troy couldn't see Eddie as he subvertly glanced around. Eddie then watched as Troy slid his hands under the rubber mat on the bar and quickly pulled out a slim stack of bills that he promptly slipped it in his coat pocket. Stunned, he watched as Troy and the barmaid, Peg, exchanged knowing looks. Then he walked out toward the casino. This was obviously not the first time the two had pulled off the little cash exchange.

Suddenly, Eddie knew there was one good thing he could do and just how to do it. He may have caused Savannah to lose Cade, but he could finally help her lose Troy Howell, too.

———— •◆• ————

Savannah was musing about how show heifers are spoiled divas that really do struggle to turn into cows. Case in point, Tiara officially retired from her show career on the way home from Denver, but it was like she really didn't know it. When Savannah and Eddie opened the gate to turn her into the pasture, Tiara literally stopped and wouldn't walk out into the muddy lot. For a week afterward she waited at the gate, even sleeping there rather than seeking to mingle with the other cows. For another week after that she came to the gate twice a day waiting for her treat or any extra attention. Now, Tiara's baby heifer had been born (and not without a little assistance) and was almost a week old. At first she didn't seem to want her at all and Savannah had to coax her into submission by pouring feed all over the tiny calf's back and putting her on the teat herself. Finally, Tiara seemed to acquiesce and cared for her little calf fairly well, if not enthusiastically.

It was one of those rare balmy February days that made spring seem close. Savannah stroked Tiara's head as the calf curled beside her mother on the hay pile. She had her camera and was taking a few shots of the pair. For a while she felt a little happy.

Eddie pulled in the drive at 4:00 just in time to help with chores.

"What are ya taking a picture of-the fact that the damn Denver Champion Female is a prima donna that has no mothering instincts whatsoever?" Eddie grumbled as he strolled up.

"That's not true at all! She loves her baby!" Eddie was just being Eddie. "Actually, I'm trying to get a cool shot for the breed magazine. I forgot to tell you that they hired me to write a series of articles about calving season and they want photos, too. It's my first writing job since college!"

"Okay, well that's cool, Savvy." Eddie said, then he surprised her by over turning an empty bucket and sitting down. "I need to talk to you about something."

"Okay, sure."

He resisted the nearly overpowering urge to flee.

"It's my fault that Cade left."

Savannah was taken aback. "What are you talking about? How?"

Eddie exhaled loudly and pushed his ball cap back while he scratched his forehead. "I sent Troy a picture of you and Cade together at Denver. The he faxed me all that marriage stuff and I paid a guy walk up and hand it to Cade."

Savannah felt like she had been punched. She stood up, but so quickly that she was light headed. Eddie quickly reached for her arm, a move that upset the bucket causing it to topple down the hill. Sensing alarm, the cow and calf jumped up, too.

Savannah whirled back to face Eddie. "Why?"

"Savannah, I honestly don't know," Eddie's voice was filled with regret. "I want you to know that I'm sorry and its been eating me alive now for over a month. Howell paid me to do it. He thinks he can hold this over your head at some point or that if you're really lonely you'll 'come to your senses' and not divorce him. It's stupid, I know, but-"

Savannah pulled back roughly and started toward the barn. Then, she whirled around and slapped Eddie firmly across the face.

The blow was direct and Eddie stumbled back, grabbing his cheek as tears sprang into his eyes. "I deserved that."

Savannah was sobbing openly now. "Eddie, *why*? We've been friends since 4-H! How could you? You know I'd never go back to Troy!"

Eddie paused; if he wimped out now, Savannah would never forgive him. "Savannah, I did it because I was jealous. It is a shitty excuse and I'm more sorry than you can ever imagine. I thought maybe you and I might, I don't know, maybe we could get together-". Watching Savannah start to shake her head, he advanced toward her. "I know, I know, that's not right for us. We're friends. But, I was pissed, too. You used me, Savannah! Every time some better lookin' guy from some other state came waltzing around you just discarded me! First it was Tripp, then Chet, and by the time it was Cade, well, damn it, I took stupid Troy up on his offer just for spite."

Savannah stopped crying suddenly and just stared at Eddie. It was as if she'd never really looked at him before. Her anger faded. Eddie was right, she had used him.

"Oh, Eddie! I'm the one who's sorry. You are so right!" she said as she leaned in and hugged him.

Eddie felt the bottom fall out of his stomach at the affection, but he hadn't come for a fight or an apology. He'd come to make things right. He gently pushed Savannah back.

"There's more, I found out something about Troy this week. Something that I think we can use to help you get rid of him."

As the afternoon faded into a chilly February evening, Eddie told Savannah about Troy's antics at the track.

Together, they devised a plan.

———————•◆•———————

Over the next two weeks Eddie spent even more time at the track, even as he drank less and less. He told Savannah they had to be sure he was right about Troy and Peg stealing from the track, so he took up residence in the booth where he'd first seen it go down. Night after night he watched as Troy indeed grabbed his little stash of money from under the mat. What Eddie learned then surprised him even more. He noticed that Troy always went to the casino as soon as he grabbed his stake, then he bet it all every time.

Why wouldn't he keep some of the money instead of risking it, Eddie wondered.

Eddie knew he would have to get something concrete pretty soon. Troy always got sloppy and let his desire to be seen as 'a wheel' get him in trouble. He was already bragging around the bar that he was on a roll, buying drinks and slapping the backs of people who neither liked him nor cared. He would eventually blow up the little scheme with Peg. Eddie told

Savannah they had to trap him before he landed in jail or got beat up by the casino boss and they couldn't benefit from using the information.

There was something fishy about the fact that Troy could suddenly pick the right nag to be the first across the line, but Eddie didn't know what.

Feeling like a bona fide private eye, Eddie had even spent a small fortune buying one of the new flip cell phones equipped with a video camera. One evening, he sat at the bar. As he pretended to leave, he placed the new phone it right in front of Peg's station near where he'd noticed that she and Troy always did their cash exchange. Eddie had set it to video and walked away not more than a minute before Troy strolled in. He watched as it videoed the whole thing, right down to Troy giving a healthy squeeze to Peg's chunky backside. Ready to move in, he approached the bar again.

"What's up Quig?" Troy remarked.

"Oh, just got me one of these damn new phones. Got to my seat and realized I left it up here. See ya around."

Troy stopped him, as Eddie expected he would. "Yeah, that little bit of money from me helping you get up to date, huh?" Troy laughed and looked smug. "Say, how's my wife? She still feeling lonely out there on the big ranch?"

"I hate to say it, since I think you're an ass, but maybe for Savannah's sake ya ought to think about talking to her," Eddie said as casually as he could. He had been baiting Troy for the last two weeks with news that Savannah lonely since the Denver disaster with Cade.

"Talk to her about what? She's got a restraining order on me!"

"How the hell should I know? I ain't married!" Eddie exclaimed, shaking his head in mock disgust. "Make her feel all warm and fuzzy and like you can take care of her or something. She's a little worried about money, too, and you appear to be up; I can't help her in that department."

Troy chortled and tossed back the last of his beer, undoubtedly on the house. "No offense, Ed, but you couldn't help my wife in any department that matters."

Eddie bristled, but Troy's unfounded confidence was amazingly easy to manipulate, Savannah had been right about that. In mock anger, Eddie rose to leave. "Listen, jerk, I was just trying to maybe help you out-a little payback from the Denver deal-but if you don't want help, well then, f-"

"No, no," Troy tugged Eddie's arm. "What did you have in mind?"

"I'll run you out by the farm tomorrow night. She'll be pissed you're there, but I'll make the case to her that you two need to kiss and make up. If my hunch is right, in her current state, she'll come around."

"Women are always so damn easy to figure out, Ed. So easy, I think even you could do it."

"Just show up tomorrow and don't act like an idiot, Howell."

Eddie called Savannah on the way home. Troy had taken the bait.

———————— ◆ ————————

Everything at the farm was in place. Savannah was dressed in a low cut top and tight jeans. Knowing Troy would be quick to overindulge, she'd made a pitcher of mixed drinks that were sweet and full of booze. Even though Eddie would plan to leave after dropping Troy off, he would quickly circle back. They both agreed that if Troy got too drunk, Savannah could get hurt. Besides, Eddie said with a wry smile, he didn't want Troy ending up dead because Savannah accidently shot him. She didn't feel very guilty when they both laughed at the thought.

Practicing with Eddie earlier in the day, she had rigged up a hidden video camera in the living room. Eddie had also shown her the cell phone video he'd taken. To her astonishment, the video showed Troy's hand reaching under the drink mat and grabbing the envelope of money. The audio of the exchange between he and Peg confirmed that he was to go place bets with the house's money and it confirmed Eddie's other suspicion about why Troy was doing so well. He was getting both the top *and* the bottom picks right, so he could win something even on the loosing horses.

Peg had the track vet it on it, too. Every time Troy came in for the cash, she also gave him the numbers of the horses in the best shape – and the worst. Troy could decently predict which ones would win and he could also bet on the poorest placing horses, too. Savannah wondered how she had been so naïve; Troy was a real snake, worse than she'd realized.

Their plan was blackmail, but it was perfect.

Knowing that Eddie and Troy would be driving in any time, Savannah downed a shot of Maker's Mark straight up. She needed to be a little loose. Troy would be characteristically easy to convince but she didn't want to risk acting too formal and fouling up.

She had only one objective: get Troy to sign the divorce papers tonight.

Finally, the lights beamed across the driveway and she heard Eddie's pick up shut off while the men came to the back door. She was in her office and they were talking loudly.

"Savannah?" Eddie called out opening the back door. "Hey, I got something I wanna say and somebody I want you to talk to."

Savannah emerged, staging a shocked expression.

"What's he doing here, Eddie?"

"I know, I know-you're gonna be mad I brought him. But don't be. You two need to talk and not fight." Eddie urged.

Troy smiled and held out a bouquet of convenience store flowers. Eddie had prepped him by saying he should approach Savannah in a conciliatory manner. Troy thought the addition of the flowers was brilliant. "Savannah, let's sit down, please I know I've done some things wrong -"

Savannah cut him off. "I just can't handle fighting right now, Troy! Not with everything I'm dealing with!" She put her hands to her face and pretended to cry.

"That's just it-I know you need somebody, Savannah!" Eddie exclaimed, moving to her side. "Please don't be mad. I'm real sorry, but I told Troy how down you've been." He cast a knowing glance at Troy.

"Come on', at least listen to what I've got to say." Troy remarked, working off Eddie's cue.

"Okay. I'll sit down, but don't think I'm giving in just because you suggested it, Eddie!" She said harshly.

"Got anything to drink around here?" Troy queried as expected.

"Hey, tell you what, I'll get you two something and then I'll split-okay?" Eddie offered as Savannah and Troy headed for the couch. Savannah settled herself right in front of the coffee table that held the picture frame - and the camcorder.

Troy never inquired as to how Eddie managed to whip up two drinks so quickly.

As planned, Eddie drove off, but parked his truck just down the road and walked back. Though Savannah said she'd need at least an hour, Eddie slipped into the house through an open window, prepared not only to do a back-up recording with his trusty new flip-phone but also to ensure Savannah's safety in case Troy got violent. By the time he got back, Savannah had her shoes off and was curled up on the couch acting convincingly sad and desperate. Troy was guzzling his cocktail and staring blatantly at Savannah's chest. Eddie winced at the scene.

Are we really that easy to fool when a woman shows a little cleavage? Eddie wondered.

Yeah, we are...

"Troy, Eddie is right, I *am* lonely, but I don't think there is any way we can make it work again," Savannah was saying as Eddie snuck into the hall that gave onto the living room and stepped into a closet. Savannah had left the door ajar to obscure Eddie from the living room but allow him enough proximity to at least get audio.

"So much has happened," she went on.

"Savannah, come on let's give it a try," Troy attempted a fake smile.

"I just have so many worries, mostly the money, Troy." Savannah leaned forward and refilled his drink. "You know this farm is all tied up in the estate. I might be able to convince my mother to give me control-I've already started talking to her about the line of credit idea you had-but it will take a little more time. I just don't know what I'll do until she comes around!"

Troy was salivating. Certainly from the way Savannah looked-he'd almost forgotten how sexy she really was- but also from the tantalizing news that she was about to talk her mother into giving up control of the farm.

This is too good to be true! I've got to act fast!

Troy put his hand on her arm and started to pull her close.

Savannah had forgotten how small his teeth were and how bad his breath stunk. His skin was so pasty it was nearly translucent. A fleeting thought of Cade and how vital and attractive he was with his sunlight skin and gold-flecked eyes and hair scampered across her mind. She forced it away.

I don't want either of them!

Swallowing barf, she sat back, trying to act cute. Right now she couldn't think about Cade; she had to do the acting job of her life.

Troy tried hard not to act annoyed. "Listen, I promise I've got enough money to keep you going for a while, at least until we get your mother talked into something."

"Troy, I know we're trying to get along, so please, *please*, don't be angry," she implored, casting down her eyes, "but we both know you're not really a very good truck salesman, so how are you getting the money?"

Then, just for fun she added: "Is Eddie loaning you money? For some reason he's got more cash lately - said he came into a couple thousand bucks."

Eddie nearly fell over at Savannah's performance and Troy's sheer ignorance. He literally had to lean against the wall to keep from dropping his new phone and rolling right out of the closet laughing.

"Yeah right!" Troy scoffed. "I'm the one giving him cash, but that's another story. Let's just say things are going well for me at the track."

"Is it that loan shark deal again? That's too dangerous!"

"No, no! I'm done messing with them, believe me. I've got something really good working – a sure thing." He reached for her again, but Savannah pulled away once more.

"I'm serious, if we're going to think about getting back together, you've got to come clean with me! Are you sure you know what you're doing? I mean, sometimes you come up with some bad plans and I just don't think you can deliver on your promises." She rolled her eyes and looked away.

"Hey, I know how to handle myself at the track, okay? But, you're kind-of wholesome, 'ya know? Sometimes you don't like to know how things work in the real world. Sometimes its just better if a man handles it." Troy sloshed more of the cocktail into his glass and attempted to act superior.

Time to go for it.

Savannah leaned forward, placing one hand along his arm.

"Troy, maybe I'm done being a good girl. Tell me how you're doing it."

That worked.

Troy recounted his ploy at the track-just the way Eddie described it.

When he finished, Troy leaned back, thoroughly amused with his cleverness.

"Now that you know, we're partners in crime. Why don't we take this upstairs?"

Savannah slowly rose from the couch, smiled bewitchingly, and stepped over to the coffee table. Troy watched her with delight.

Is she going to strip?

Instead, to his horror, she pulled the video camera out from behind an empty picture frame.

"What the f-?"

"Troy, its time for a divorce. I've taped this and I will use it against you. But, I don't have to. Get up, sign the divorce papers and get the hell out of my life."

"You've gotta be sh-" Troy was confused and his head was foggy. But something was going terribly wrong.

Eddie walked out of the closet.

"He's got it recorded on his cell phone, too."

"You two were in cahoots?" Still stunned, Troy stumbled to his feet. "So what! So 'ya heard me making up some story - that doesn't mean shit."

"It does when you couple it with this." Eddie played back the video of Troy and Peg.

Troy lunged at Eddie, nearly grabbing him, but Savannah tripped him. Troy sprawled across the rug, but quickly rolled over, ready to get up and fight. The cold steel of Savannah's double barrel stopped him.

"Two choices," Savannah's voice had a ragged edge. "I shoot you or you sign."

"You wouldn't, you little b-"

"Believe me, I'd really like to, but I might not, who knows? But I will keep you away from Eddie long enough for him to drive out of here and go straight to the track. Either way you are screwed."

Eddie ran to the front door and clamored into Savannah's waiting pick up truck. He held up the phone as he fired the ignition.

Troy started to whimper. "Eddie, buddy, you'll get me killed if you do that! Come back here. We can work this out, Man!"

"Sign the papers and leave, Troy," was all Eddie said.

As Savannah watched, gun cocked, Troy Howell finally made a wise choice.

~ SEVENTEEN ~

Springtime Renewal

"Savannah, honey, you've paid alright, just not with cash," Jessica Morgan said as Savannah told her that she was able to get rid of Troy Howell without giving him any money or by selling off a piece of ground. "You want to tell me how?"

"Someday maybe."

The two Morgan women were on the porch, a spring breeze rustling around them. Jessica had opened a bottle of expensive cabernet and was pouring it into glasses.

"Well, its time you moved on and quit being so low. I don't know who you were moping over after Denver, but I bet it wasn't that sweet Chet - good as he looked-"

"I don't want to talk about it, Mother," Savannah rolled her eyes. Sighing, she sipped the wine. "It didn't make sense, it wouldn't have worked."

"Oh, Savannah, now you're being naïve about love. Honey, it never makes sense."

Savannah rolled her eyes again. Jessica smiled wanly.

"Well, I have something to admit to you. I'm dating Roland Madsen."

"Yeah, I figured."

"Well, you probably did, but you didn't figure on the fact that I think that is why your Dad had the heart attack in Kansas City."

Savannah's heart froze. "What are you talking about?"

Jessica leaned forward, twirling the large glass between her slender fingers. "You know that your Dad and I had been separated for years. He was okay with it, but I wasn't. I wanted to move on, to be free, but I stayed because I felt like I owed it to him. Finally, things with Roland – we've known each other for decades – got to the point where it was time. He'd been so patient."

"You told Dad you wanted a divorce."

"Yes, the morning of the show," the words were barely audible. Jessica began to cry.

Savannah stood, walked to the edge of the porch, then thought better of it. Turning back, she sat down next to Jessica and embraced her. "There is no way that Dad dying was your fault."

"Thank you," Jessica whispered.

———————— • ◆ • ————————

In the month since she was finally free from Troy, Savannah had thought a lot about what had made her stay. She thought a lot about the farm and her future on it. Jessica said she had to decide for herself how to manage it and if it meant enough to her to struggle through it. She assured her mother that it did.

Savannah spent a lot of time thinking of ways she could improve cash flow, modernize, and make the operation more efficient. She also decided to generate a little money with writing, a love she had neglected for too long. It was the bright spot in her life. The act of writing, first in a notebook late at night and then early before dawn had helped her navigate the upheaval of the last several months. Then, she began writing in earnest writing on the old desktop. Though it needed an update, at this point a Word processing program and a memory stick were enough to begin.

She wrote stories about the farm and about her thoughts. And, poems, too. She'd taken a few farm pictures and sent them off to breed magazines and already seen them published. Her first check for $50 might as well have been $5,000 for all the encouragement it had given her.

Mostly, Savannah spent time thinking about the fact that her entire life she'd relied on men, not because she necessarily trusted them, or even because she loved them; she had relied on men because she had never chosen to trust herself.

First, there had been her Dad. Even though they struggled to get along, she had let him tell her what to do because it was easier than trying to talk with him about her own independent ideas. He was bullheaded and chauvinist. As she grew up, it became easier just to play along than argue his point. She wanted to be around the cows bad enough that biting her tongue and letting him have his way had been the price.

Even though Troy was a jerk, she had to admit that she had relied on him, too. She'd let Troy feed her weaknesses and give in to her darkest moments. Troy enabled Savannah to live a mediocre life and to hold back when she wanted to take a risk or try to achieve her dreams. He always made a point to remind her of what she couldn't do or wasn't good at. He'd limited her and he'd insulted her, but she'd let him.

Life with both Troy and her dad had been easier than growing up and seeking to really *live*.

She had relied on Eddie. She'd used Eddie, too, and that had been wrong, probably even cruel at times. Savannah couldn't be mad at him. He had given in to jealousy and helped foul things up with Cade, but he was still her one true friend.

And Chet. Bless his heart, Chet. She hoped he'd find a woman to love him as much as he deserved to be loved.

Most of all, she had relied on Cade.

Cade Champion had walked into her life and swept her away with a passion that she never dreamt was possible. Cade had taken care of everything when she was most afraid. He had gotten her stock clipped and looking better than she and Eddie ever could. He had set up the heifer sale deal with Clint. For all she knew, with his connections he might have finagled Tiara's win, too, though she hadn't heard any gossip to support that notion. Cade was so good looking and so capable that he'd been almost unreal. Maybe he was.

But God she missed him.

The physical part of him, his smile, the boyish way he flirted, and the masculine way he took charge of things that scared her were all part of the problem! Her attraction to him had been stunning, almost *debilitating*, she realized now. Maybe it was just too dangerous to feel that way about another person.

Besides, in reality, she didn't really even know Cade Champion. They'd spent less than a week together but he had absolutely broken her heart. That he apparently didn't miss her the way she missed him made Savannah hurt and angry. She had made *way* too many mistakes with men, mostly because she'd relied on them to make the decisions in life and in love.

Or what passed for love, but wasn't.

Clint said that Cade had a tough childhood in some ways, that his mother was a distant floozy and that he'd had 'an incident' once where he did something stupid and almost wound up married to a very, very wrong woman. Clint said he was gun shy and since Savannah hadn't been honest with him, Cade probably just wasn't able to deal with it. Clint apparently had business in Indianapolis every three to four weeks because he found reason to visit her often. After the one time they talked about Cade, neither mentioned it again. Savannah wasn't sure if Clint was trying to date her or just be a friend and it didn't matter. She liked Clint, though his arrogance could be abrasive at times. Still, she felt no attraction to him; nobody compared to Cade.

It wasn't worth pining for Cade!

If he had really cared for her, if he had *loved* her, he would have reached out. She played the scenarios over and over for weeks wondering why he never called to listen or to try and understand. He had just left. If he had really cared that much, he would had fought for her, but he didn't. If he had fallen as hard for her as she did for him then he would not have walked away without a trace.

But he had.

What Jessica had said was right; she had to discover what she really wanted. She respected her mother now more than ever and was sorry that Jessica had lived with so much guilt over her own unhappy marriage. Still, that had been Jessica's choice. Savannah had her own ability to make choices and it was time she started doing just that. She was moving on and she was going to be okay. It was time to shine, on her own.

Today she had made the first step in building relationships with men for the right reasons. She had offered Eddie a partnership. It felt good and fair when she made Eddie the deal of 30% of sales instead of only being hired help.

"Let's just start with this year and see how it goes. If you don't like it, we won't renew. It will be up to us to make good decisions, together," Savannah had suggested when she approached him with the idea.

"What about shows?" Eddie had asked.

"Sure, I'll pay all your expenses when we're at shows."

"Including beer?"

"You can still have all the beer you want, Eddie, but you've got to act like an owner now, so less running around and staying out too late," Savannah admonished.

"And Crown, you'd wouldn't cheap out and buy Old Crow?" By then he was smiling, obviously pleased.

"Only top shelf for us, Eddie," Savannah said as they shook hands.

~ EPILOGUE ~

It was spring and Savannah felt good. She'd been outside all day gardening. Eddie had sheared off the cow's winter hair and the calves were looking really nice. Stepping into the kitchen, she opened a bottle of wine and poured herself a glass, then decided she would make a salad from the greens she just picked. Absently, she noticed the blinking light on the answering machine and hit play.

The voice on the line stopped her cold.

"Savannah," began the masculine baritone. Her body instantly recognized the sound.

A pause.

"Savannah," came the voice again as her knees buckled and she reached for the back of a chair.

"Savannah, it's Cade. Cade Champion. I, well, uh, I guess I called to say hi. No, I mean, I really hope we can talk. No, I mean, I need to see you."

Cade paused again. Savannah's pulse quickened.

"Hey," Cade said, the familiar lilt to his voice, his mocking tone milder, but there. "I wanted you to be the first to know, I finally got a cell phone."

As Cade began to relay the numbers, instinctively Savannah reached for a pen to jot them down. In her shock, she hadn't hear them all. Her hand hovered over the machine to push replay.

Something made her hesitate. Somewhere deep inside the resolve to take care of herself came surging through the alluring sounds of Cade's voice.

Savannah straightened and took a sip of wine.

She pushed delete.

The End

Acknowledgements

The publication of *Championship Drive* is the realization of my longest held dream. I've wanted to write and publish a novel since my earliest memories of reading books at the library. *Championship Drive*, through the development of its characters, has also allowed me the gift of sharing many of my own hopes and disappointments in the livestock business. I have to admit, there isn't anything I love more than raising and showing cattle.

I wish to thank the seed stock industry for its wealth of wonderful stories, colorful people, and great experiences. I am inspired by livestock enthusiasts of all ages that are driven to be successful in breeding and exhibiting their stock. It's a passion so many of us hold dear; it is my hope that *Championship Drive* honors that spirit of competition and excellence.

Once I started admitting that I planned to publish 'my cow-showing novel', I was stunned by the encouragement from so many friends. I think many of you just hope you'll end up being a character in the book, though! Still, thank you for letting me know that, yes, people *really will* want to read it. I hope you enjoy *Championship Drive* as much as I've enjoyed creating it.

Two very, very special women contributed to the development of this work - my mother, Ann Potter and my grandmother, Dorothy Willard. These ladies braved the early drafts and edited this book. They didn't always agree about the plot, either! I'll let them share which one thought the book should have more explicit detail in the romantic scenes…

Their guidance with *Championship Drive*, as with all of my life, is precious to me. Thank you, Grandma and Mom.

Most of all I want to thank my husband, Cary Aubrey, who asked simply: 'why not now?' Cary gave me the courage to publish *Championship Drive* and to press on when I thought about wimping out. Cary keeps *our* cows fed, our home warm, and my showing dreams alive. I'm grateful to you, Sugar, and I love you.